Hope Rising

Hope Rising

Messianic Promise

BY

Jeffrey D. Johnson

FOREWORD BY

Eric E. Walker

WIPF & STOCK · Eugene, Oregon

Wipf & Stock
An Imprint of Wipf and Stock Publishers
199 W. 8th Ave., Suite 3
Eugene, OR 97401

www.wipfandstock.com

PAPERBACK ISBN: 978-1-6667-5574-9
HARDCOVER ISBN: 978-1-6667-5575-6
EBOOK ISBN: 978-1-6667-5576-3

11/01/22

Contents

Foreword

EVERY YEAR ON THE first night of Hanukkah, one of our family traditions was to open a brand-new jigsaw puzzle for the family to assemble with the goal of completing it before the eighth night. When we were young, the puzzles were maybe 200 pieces and fairly simple, but as we got older, the puzzles became more complex and there are now 2,000–3,000 pieces. We always knew what we were trying to assemble as the picture was on the outside of the box. There was always the mad scramble to find the pieces with the straight edges so we could outline the framework, but after that, it became more complex finding what fit where.

Imagine if the puzzle you were attempting to assemble came wrapped in a plain black wrapper with no indication as to what the final assembled puzzle would look like. The package contained no instructions, no piece count, and no way to pour out the pieces on a card table and work as a family to fit the pieces neatly together.

My dear friend, brother, scholar, and counselor, Dr. Jeffrey Johnson has been gathering puzzle pieces for decades and, in this new work, has created a literary tapestry that weaves together smaller sections of individual biblical puzzles that seemingly stood alone. As Dr. Jeff began to lay out these puzzle pieces, he began to see the outer edges forming and the framework taking shape.

There is an old saying, "A picture is worth a thousand words," but in the case of *Hope Rising: Messianic Promise*, these thousands of words paint a picture beyond compare. That mysterious puzzle wrapped in a plain black wrapper transformed multiple puzzles into one cohesive picture of our Messiah. What took us eight days to assemble at Hanukkah, took Dr. Jeff a lifetime.

His wit and wisdom, combined with his deep compassion for his fellow man, shines through the pages of this wonderful literary tapestry. Dr. Jeff has taken us from the outer edges to the sweet center of this portrait of God's love for all mankind through his gift of Messiah.

If you or a loved one have been searching for how the Bible fits together and have been overwhelmed by the complexity of the puzzle pieces, this book will take the black and white pieces of the Bible and turn them into living color.

Dr. Jeff is a blessing to all who know him, and this is his invitation to join him in the life that God desires for you. I am honored and blessed to know him and love him and thank God for the gift of this new work.

Rabbi Eric E. Walker

Executive Director/On-Air Host, Igniting a Nation Ministries

Author of *Etz Chaim—Lessons Learned from the Tree of Life*, *The Codist*, *The Seven Laws of Abundant Living*, and *3:15—The Genesis of All Prophecy*

Introduction

THE FOLLOWING IS A compilation of lectures given in churches, universities, and study groups. Some have been previously published as booklets and others as teaching emails. These lectures outline the greatest hope in history—the story of God's love and purpose for humanity.

This book is for your grandmother, and other family members to read, and for all the people in your life who believe in, or are searching for, the hope found only in Jesus the Messiah.

No claim is made for originality, but I am deeply grateful for the help I received from the many resources in my personal library and other scholarly wells of inspiration found in the footnotes and bibliography. May God's peace ascend in your heart as you search for meaning and the promises found in Messiah!

Dr. Jeff

President
Israel Today Ministries
Arlington, Texas

——— Chapter 1 ———

The Fingerprint of God

THERE ARE THOSE WHO argue that Moses did not write the Torah. However, for our purposes today, we will assume that Moses penned the words. In the introduction of the first paragraph of Genesis, Moses begins, *Bereshit bara Elohim*—"In the beginning God created."

Elohim is the sovereign architect, the Judge who declares. The word *created* in Hebrew is *Bara*—something only God can do—that is create or creating something out of nothing.

God spoke, "Let there be" (*yehi*)—a *cohortative* form or mood, expressing desire or wish, a declaration.

God said, "Light" and there was Light.

God made the "firmament" and there was firmament.

God called the dry land "earth," and it became earth.

God said, God made, God called, God created—all in the first paragraph, in the second paragraph, third paragraph, and fourth and fifth paragraphs.

God said, "And it was so" or *Va-yehi ken*—And it was "YES." Then Moses adds, "That it was good" or *Ki-Tov*.

Notice it was "A" first day (*Yom Echad*—One day); "A" second day (*Yom Sheni*); "A" third day (*Yom shelishi*); "A" fourth day (*Yom revii*); "A" fifth day (*Yom chamishi*).

Now, in the sixth paragraph of Genesis, there is a paradigm shift taking place. Moses writes, "Then God said, "Let Us make man in Our image, according to Our likeness" (1:26).

The three words *Let us make (nah-say)* is the *jussive form* or mood, expressing *a command*—which is different from "Let there be" or *y' hee*. The

1

change tells us something profound is about to happen. God is deliberately doing something here; something great is unfolding.

Moses not only writes, ". . . and it was so (and it was *Yes*)," he also pens, "And, behold, it was *very* good" (*ve-hee-nay tov* ma-od). Then he writes, "*The* sixth day (*Yom* Ha-*shee shee*)" The definite article *The* is used in contrast to the indefinite article *A*. The use of the plural pronoun in "Let us" opens the door to the plurality in the Godhead, as was true with the word *Elohim*.

The rabbis teach that God was speaking to angels—however, the text *never* indicates angels were part of the conversation. If God had consulted, it would have said so, as in the case of 1 Kgs 22:19–23 where God consulted with the heavenly court about doing something.[1]

The words *In our image* in Hebrew is one word *betzalmeinu* and refers to the original image or imitation. This same word is also used of idols.[2] In the ancient Near East, the ruling king was often described as the "image" or the "likeness" of a god which served to elevate the monarch above ordinary mortals. In the Bible, this idea became democratized. *Every* human being is created "in the image of God"; each bears the stamp of royalty.

Thus, the description of mortals as "in the image of God" makes humankind the symbol of God's presence on earth.[3]

This preamble ("Let us make man") indicates that man was created with great deliberation—that man was brought into being with the deepest involvement of Divine Providence and wisdom.[4]

Rashi stated, "In our image, or in Our mold meaning that God had prepared the mold with which He would now shape man. . . .Throughout the chapter, God brought all things into being with an utterance, but He created man with His own hands as it were."[5]

"According (after) our likeness" is one Hebrew word *kidmuteinu* which means "a model" or "a copy." This also emphasizes the uniqueness of human beings.

> "God created man in His own image,
> in the image of God He created him;
> male and female He created them" (1:27 (NASB)).

1. Fruchtenbaum, *Book of Genesis*, 56.

2. Fruchtenbaum, *Book of Genesis*, 56.

3. Lieber, *Etz Hayim*, 9.

4. Scherman, *Chumash*, 8.

5. Scherman, *Chumash*, 8–9.

God created man—He created woman—He created them. The word *bara* is used three times to emphasize that a high point, a profound moment, was reached here. (Remember *bara* is a word only used of God and of the work that only God can do. It is never used with anything man does).

The prophet Isaiah declares, "Thus says God the Lord, who created the heavens, and stretched them out; who gives breath to the people on it, I, the Lord will hold your hand, and will keep you" (Isa. 42:5–6).

We can see in this text that God has great concern and truly cares for people. If God can create "the stars also" in all their glory and magnificence, imagine the significance of human beings?

Mindful

David writes, "What is man, that you are *mindful* of him?" (Ps. 8:4–5). The term *mindful* suggests that God is continually thinking about people. We are constantly on His mind.

David also states, with extreme pathos, "I am poor and needy; yet the Lord *thinks* about me" (Ps. 40:17). The word *thinks* has the idea of "to regard and value."

The Apostle Paul states, "For in Him we live and move and have our being" (Acts 17:28).

In Genesis 2:7, Moses gives us an account of God creating Adam: "Then the LORD God *formed* the man of dust from the ground and breathed into his nostrils the breath of life, and the man became a living soul." The verb *formed* or *va-yitzer* is often used in the Bible to describe the activity of a potter (*yotzer*). *Yitzer* is used in the following: a potter shaping clay (Isa. 29:16; Jer. 18:1–17); goldsmiths who make idols (Isa. 44:9; Hab. 2:18); regarding the shaping of Messiah's body in the womb (Isa. 49:5); also, where God forms hearts (Ps. 33:15) and the eye (Ps. 94:9); and when God formed man (Ps. 119:73).

In Genesis 2:7, *Yitzer* (*formed*) is used, whereas, in chapter one, *Bara* (*created*) was used. *Bara* emphasizes something only God can do—that is create or creating something out of *nothing*. He spoke, and it was so. In contrast, *Yitzer* (*formed*) emphasizes "to mold" or "shape by design" out of *something*—"dust." Although, man was created out of something, it was something only God could do.

God spoke the whole universe, and all therein, into existence. However, in Genesis 2, He did not speak and say, "Let there be man." The text

3

implies that with His own hands, as it were, He created or formed Adam! Created in the divine image, both man and woman were created on the sixth day, and both were created in the image of God.

The next part of verse 7 says, "Breathed into his nostrils the breath of life." The breath of life deals with the immaterial part of man. In Hebrew, it is *nishmat chaim*. This is the *neshamah*, or the breath of God, and the word is used twenty-five times in the Old Testament. God's breath brings animation, causing Adam to become a *living soul*. In Job 32:8, it is recorded, "But it is the spirit in man, the breath of the Almighty, that makes him understand." God's breath brings spiritual understanding. Therefore, the result is moral capacity.[6]

The Hebrew word *ruach* (spirit, wind) is used of God, man, animal, and idols. The word *neshamah* or *breath* is used only of God and man, except once, where it is used of animals. It is this breath of God, the *neshamah*, that produced the life of Adam. In Genesis 7:22, the *neshamah* is also found in animals, but only to Adam is it directly given. Only of Adam does it say that "God breathed into his nostrils the breath of life," making Adam (human beings) somewhat distinct from the animal kingdom. This means that not only is man physical, man is also spirit.

The result of this breathing in of the breath of God was "that Adam became a living soul (*nephesh chayah*)." Therefore, a human being's uniqueness does not lie in the fact of the *breath of life* as such, because the same words are used of the animal kingdom. However, our uniqueness lies in the fact that we have the image of God and the animal kingdom does not.[7]

"So God created man in his own image, in the image of God he created him; male and female he created them" (Gen. 1:27).

Rashi, the revered Jewish sage, stated, "Thus, the human being is a combination of the earthly and the divine."[8] And He blew into his nostrils the soul of life. God thus made Man out of both lower (earthly) and upper (heavenly) matter: his body from the dust and his soul from the spirit.[9] The Jewish sages state from *The Chumash* or "one who blows, blows from within himself," indicating that man's soul is part of God's essence.[10]

---

6. Fruchtenbaum, *Book of Genesis*, 74.

7. Fruchtenbaum, *Book of Genesis*, 74–75.

8. Lieber, *Etz Hayim*, 13.

9. Scherman, *Chumash*, 11.

10. Sherman, *Chumash*, 11.

The word *soul* derives from the Hebrew root *Nephesh* which has several connotations, according to Al Novak in *Hebrew Honey*:

a. Breath, or the Principle of Life: When this breath is absent there is death. At death, the spirit is departed.

b. Mind and rationality: The idea is that the soul not only discovers the trustworthy but persuades the whole person to place his trust in it or cast his all upon it.

c. The seat of affections, feelings and emotions: The soul, which the Lord breathed into the body, feels after the Lord and, upon discovering Him, is moved to rejoice in Him.

d. It signifies a person: That which can love or hate; that which can sing or be sad; that which can be excited by the right or by the wrong makes up the total personality.[11]

Benjamin Blech states, "The soul came from God, and it returns to spend eternity with its divine source.[12] Nahum Sarna declares, "[Humans] are different from the beasts of the field by [their] intellect, free will, self-awareness, consciousness of the existence of others, conscience, responsibility, and self-control."[13]

I tell my students, and I tell you—"You are here this moment, this second, this minute, this hour, on this planet, in this solar system, in this universe, for a reason—you are no mistake. God makes no mistake!" Being created "in the image of God" implies that human life is infinitely precious.[14] David exclaimed, "I am fearfully and wonderfully made" (Ps. 139:14).

Both man and woman were created on the sixth day and both were created in the image of God, thus, human beings are **the fingerprint of God.**

"Thou hast made us for thyself, O Lord,
and our heart is restless until it finds its rest in thee."

—Augustine, *Confessions*

11. Novak, *Hebrew Honey*, 242.

12. Blech, *Secrets*, 129.

13. Sarna, *Understanding Genesis*, 16.

14. Sarna, *Understanding Genesis*, 16.

Chapter 2

The Passionate Sacrifice

The Binding of Isaac: Genesis 22

The Preparation

"Few narrative sections of the (Old Testament) have been subjected to as much comment and study as the 'Akedah' (or) the binding of Isaac."[1] Its subject matter ranges from the God who tests . . . to the man who is tested . . . from the nature of faith . . . to the demands it makes . . . and it considers many other questions as well . . . There are many levels of meaning.[2]

In this chapter, we will focus our attention on the messianic presage it presents.

"It took the Lord (approximately) sixty years to prepare Abraham for this climactic event."[3] From the promise in Genesis 12 to the birth of Isaac in Genesis 21 was a period of twenty-five years. From Isaac's birth to this most salient episode was a time frame of over thirty years. During those years, Abraham and Sarah confused and misinterpreted God's promise many times. As we reflect upon their story recorded in Genesis, we will find failure as well as victory. This was all part of their journey and purpose, and it did not take God by surprise. "The Lord never does put us to the test until we are ready for it."[4] There is never a testing, trial, or hardship that comes our way that God has not prepared us to go through. Neither is the Lord ever in a hurry to accomplish that which He has started in our lives.

1. Plaut, *The Torah*, 203.
2. Plaut, *The Torah*, 203.
3. DeHaan, *Adventures in Faith*, 153.
4. DeHaan, *Adventures in Faith*, 153.

Abraham is now ready; let's look at his story.

"Now it came to pass after these things that God tested Abraham, and said to him, 'Abraham!' And he said, 'Here I am'" (Genesis 22:1).

Ready Lord!

Verse 1

Here I am means "ready, Lord," "at your service," "yes, sir," "at once." This reflects submission. After many years he is now a yielded vessel at the feet of a holy God. Now comes the ultimate test.

"Then He said, Take now your son, your only son Isaac, whom you love, and go to the land of Moriah; and offer him there as a burnt offering on one of the mountains of which I shall tell you" (Genesis 22:2).

Your Only Son

"The original Hebrew language is far more tender than this. It should read this way: 'And he said, Take now thy son, thine only son Isaac . . . whom thou lovest.'"[5] "Abraham is reminded of the dearest possession of his life."[6]

The idea here is that Abraham is to do this himself . . . it "rules out the idea of others sharing in the test."[7] "Luther and others may not be far from the truth when he suggested that the patriarch told nothing of his purpose to Sarah."[8]

Verse 2

"Only" son (Hebrew, *Yachid*, "the unique one, one and only"), it has the same idea as "only begotten." Isaac was the "promised (one) child that was foretold."

5. DeHaan, *Adventures in Faith*, 156.
6. Thomas, *Genesis*, 195.
7. Leupold, *Exposition*, 620.
8. Leupold, *Exposition*, 620.

"Somehow, we approach this scene with fear and trembling . . . we can (almost) hear God saying to us what He said to Moses . . . 'Take off thy shoes, for the ground whereon thou standest is holy ground.'"[9]

God says to Abraham: "Take now your son, your only son Isaac . . . and offer him . . . on one of the mountains of which I shall tell you." "As far as the record goes, Abraham believed God . . . (and) was willing to make the supreme sacrifice, to take his son and to slay him upon the altar, in order that he might please Him who called him from darkness into light."[10] That reminds us most vividly of John 3:16:

"For God so loved the world, that He gave His only begotten Son . . . "

Isaiah brings a clearer focus.

"Yet it pleased the Lord to bruise Him; He has put Him to grief"
(Isaiah 53:10).

"Your only son." "What does God mean, 'your only son'? Abraham had other sons. He had Ishmael who was born thirteen years prior to Isaac. He had many sons afterward(s) . . . God, however, recognized as a fit sacrifice only one son, the miraculously born . . . supernaturally given . . . promised son . . . Isaac is the only one whom God will recognize . . . all the blessing that will come upon the rest of the children must come through this one particular son. God also gave His only son . . . but He, too, had many other sons. We read in the Book of Job about a great host of angelic beings, called the sons of God. Then, too, Adam is called by Luke, a son of God. And we, by our new creation, are the sons of God.

But angels could not fill the requirement for the substitute, and Adam could not pay for his own sin, and we . . . (are) unable to meet God's requirement. There was (and is) only ONE, God's only Son, who was fit to become the substitute for our sin."[11]

In Abraham, we see the love of God which surpasses our understanding.

"Moriah (eight centuries later) became the site of the temple where all the sacrifices were offered . . . where God rent the veil in two (so) that free access might be (made) for all the people of God . . . ."[12] This is indeed the

9. DeHaan, *Adventures in Faith*, 156.

10. DeHaan, *Adventures in Faith*, 156–57.

11. DeHaan, *Adventures in Faith*, 157–58.

12. Barnhouse, *Genesis*, 197.

same area in which our Lord was crucified for our sins. This is a beautiful picture that the Holy Spirit gives us centuries before the Lord came.

Sleepless Night

"So Abraham rose early in the morning and saddled his donkey, and took two of his young men with him, and Isaac his son; and he split the wood for the burnt offering, and arose and went to the place of which God had told him" (Genesis 22:3).

Verse 3

"Early in the morning." I don't believe Abraham slept that night. Perhaps he wrestled and agonized with God as he did for Sodom and Gomorrah, even with greater pathos. I find an interesting parallel in the fact that our Lord "early, (the) morning of His crucifixion, after the evening in the Passover chamber . . . came (to) Gethsemane."[13] The Scriptures tell us that He, Jesus, "began to be troubled and deeply distressed" (Mark 14:33). There He agonized, wrestling with His Father and praying, "Father, if it is Your will, take this cup away from Me; nevertheless not My will, but Yours, be done" (Luke 22:42).

It is appropriate that the Lord went to Gethsemane. Gethsemane means "wine press or oil press."

On that fateful morning of betrayal and arrest, the record tells us that Jesus "being in agony, He prayed more earnestly. Then His sweat became like great drops of blood falling down to the ground" (Luke 22:44). He was being "pressed," yielding to His Father's will and purpose. Abraham, too.

On the Third Day

"Then on the third day Abraham lifted his eyes and saw the place afar off. And Abraham said to his young men, 'Stay here with the donkey; and the lad and I will go yonder and worship, and we will come back to you. So Abraham took the wood of the burnt offering, and laid it on Isaac his son; and he took the fire in his hand, and a knife; and the two of them went together" (Genesis 22:4–6).

13. DeHaan, *Adventures in Faith*, 160.

Verses 4–6

"Saw the place afar off." "His vision included more than a mountain in the land of Moriah . . . . He saw past the deed to the resurrection . . . past the type to the fulfillment . . . past Isaac to the (Messiah). The New Testament will not permit any other interpretation.

"By faith Abraham, when he was tested, offered up Isaac, and he who had received the promises offered up his only begotten son, of whom it was said, 'In Isaac your seed shall be called,' concluding that God was able to raise him up, even from the dead . . . " (Hebrews 11:17–19).

Our Lord reminded the Pharisees of this fact, 'Your father Abraham rejoiced to see My day: and he saw it and was glad' (John 8:56)."[14]

Verse 5–6

"Worship" means to "bow low," to "yield," to "submit."

"We will come back to you." Abraham fully believed that God would indeed raise Isaac from the dead due to the fact that God's Word is true. God stated that through the promised child "all the families of the earth shall be blessed" (Genesis 12:3).

No Man Takes My Life

Notice he *"took the wood . . . and laid it on Isaac his son."* Abraham was 100 years older than Isaac. Isaac could easily have resisted but did not. Here is a true picture of our Lord, who said,

"Therefore my Father loves me, because I lay down My life that I may take it again. No one takes it from Me, but I lay it down of Myself. I have power to lay it down, and I have power to take it again. This command have I received from my Father" (John 10:17–18).

"Abraham would have been no match for Isaac, if he had resisted, . . . but Isaac bore the wood, as Christ bore the cross."[15]

"Fire and knife." As the wood points to the cross, "fire in the Scripture has the meaning of judgment. Again and again fire and flame speak of judgment in preparation for the love of God. It was a flame and a sword that guarded Eden . . . . It was fire which destroyed Sodom and Gomorrah . . .

14. Barnhouse, *Genesis*, 199.

15. Barnhouse, *Genesis*, 200.

and very significantly the place of eternal judgment is called the lake of fire. We have here then a picture of the cross and the judgment which was to fall upon another Son because of the sin of humanity."[16]

Knife—a butcher knife, a sacrificial knife, used in sacrificing animals. "A knife in Scripture speaks of the Word of God."[17]

> *"For the word of God is living and powerful, and sharper than any two-edged sword . . . " (Hebrews 4:12).*

"God foreknew and foresaw that man would sin. Even before man was created, God had ready a plan of salvation which included the death of His Son. John in Revelation tells us that Jesus is the 'Lamb slain from before the foundation of the world.' (Revelation 13:8) You see, (Jesus) came in the fullness of time, according to the promise and according to the Word of God, with a knife in His hand."[18]

"Two of them went together." "The narrative gives free play to our imagination as it pictures (the) father and son proceeding step (by) step up the hill."[19] "Here we have perfect agreement. Abraham did not have to force his son to climb up. . . . They were both agreed and of one mind."[20] The son was obedient unto death.

> *" . . . He was led as a lamb to the slaughter, and as a sheep before its shearers is silent, So He opened not His mouth" (Isaiah 53:7).*

"But Isaac spoke to Abraham his father and said, 'My father!' And he said, 'Here I am, my son.' Then he said, 'Look, the fire and the wood, but where is the lamb for a burnt offering?' And Abraham said, 'My son, God will provide for himself the lamb for a burnt offering.' So the two of them together" (Genesis 22:7–8).

Where is the Lamb?

Verses 7–8

The two of them went together. But Isaac spoke.

---

16. DeHaan, *Adventures in Faith*, 162.
17. DeHaan, *Adventures in Faith*, 162.
18. DeHaan, *Adventures in Faith*, 162.
19. Leupold, *Exposition*, 625.
20. DeHaan, *Adventures in Faith*, 162.

The idea is that the father and son walked in oppressive silence until Isaac asked the question, "Where is the lamb, Father?" Isaac knew what was necessary for sacrifice. Abraham's response is full of pathos. The question pierced Abraham's heart like a knife. Trembling with great apprehension, he said, "Behold me, my son" (or "Yes, my son" or "Here am I, my son.").

"God will provide for Himself the lamb." Jehovah-Jireh, 'the Lord will see to it,' 'provide,' 'look out for' or 'choose.' The Lord will provide . . . .

"My son" is an expression of tenderness as though Abraham was sparing Isaac from unnecessary pain and detail. Abraham fully intended to sacrifice his son, to spill his blood, to burn his body. He did not know there would be a ram in the bushes. He left this painful issue with a merciful God. Abraham's presage was nothing less than profound—"The Lord will see to it; The Lord will provide; *The Lord will provide Himself . . .* " He knew that "(God) Himself is going to pay the price . . . He Himself is going to be the Lamb in the person of His Son. What a marvelous truth of the atonement! When no one else could pay, God said, 'I'll pay the price.' That answer satisfied Isaac . . . 'and the two of them went together.'"[21]

Sleep-Walking

"Then they came to the place which God had told him. And Abraham built an altar there and placed the wood in order; and he bound Isaac his son and laid him on the altar, upon the wood. And Abraham stretched out his hand and took the knife to slay his son" (Genesis 22:9–10).

Verses 9–10

Notice "the staccato phrases that heighten the tension. (The short, abrupt, pithy statements) . . . . Abraham seems to move 'like a sleep-walker.'"[22] Abraham was numb, much like when we receive bad news or learn about the death of a loved one. Abraham actually binds his son. Isaac submits to this act in total otherworldly confidence in his father. "A confidence built upon a complete understanding and a deep love which knew that the father could wish his son no harm."[23]

21. DeHaan, *Adventures in Faith*, 164.

22. Plaut, *The Torah*, 206.

23. Leupold, *Exposition*, 627.

"In Leviticus, where the continuing sacrifices are begun, we discover that the pieces of wood were laid in order upon the altar (Leviticus 1:7) and that a horizontal bolt of fire from the Holy of Holies ignited the wood and consumed the offering (Leviticus 9:24). God Himself furnished the material and the fire (that) consumed the sacrifice, for He Himself (will) put His Son to death (Isaiah 53:10) . . . 'it pleased the Lord to bruise Him . . .'"[24]

The Sacred Moment

Verse 10

"The center of the scene shifts from the father to son and back to the father, for the Lord is emphasizing the fact that both were going to the sacrifice together, obeying, yielding, co-operating even as the heavenly Father and the Lord Jesus Christ did at Calvary. With the consent of Isaac, Abraham binds him . . . and lays him on the altar . . . ."[25]

Another important point is that on top of the mountain there was no one around except Abraham and Isaac. "When they went to the place of sacrifice, they took two men along . . . but when they came to the mountain, Abraham said, 'You two stay behind . . . .' When that awful moment came . . . Abraham lifted up his . . . (knife) . . . there was no one around, no one to witness it, no one to see it . . . (WHY?) The scene was too sacred, too holy . . . Do you see the picture?

When the Son of God went up to Calvary, His Father went with Him, and was right there at Calvary, holding His Son's hand as He walked up the mountain . . . . But there were two other men also, one on the right hand, and one on the left . . . . (Then) the time came for the sacrifice, the time for that holy scene which no eye might behold. Just as Abraham denied the two men who went with them an opportunity to see the actual transaction, so also did God . . . . (You see) for when the time came, every one must be shut out, and no one must see. From the sixth hour, 'there was darkness over the whole earth until the ninth hour.' (Matthew 27:45) For three hours no human eye beheld what took place on the Cross of Calvary. The Father snuffed out the lights of heaven, He pulled down the shades of the sky, separated Himself with His Son alone."[26]

24. Barnhouse, *Genesis,* 201.

25. Barnhouse, *Genesis,* 202.

26. DeHaan, *Adventures in Faith,* 164–65.

"At the end of those three black hours we hear a cry, as the Father seems to say to His Son, 'I've got to go now . . . . The rest of the way you will have to go all alone . . . by yourself . . . all alone.' And (then) there comes the piercing cry from the Son of God upon the cross, (Eli, Eli, Lama Sabachthani) 'My God, My God, why hast thou forsaken me?' Alone He had to die and pay the price, so that you and I would never have to be alone . . . so that we would never have to experience the loneliness of being forever forsaken."[27] At that very moment, He bore our sin.

Isaac Died

"But the angel of the Lord called to him from heaven and said, 'Abraham, Abraham!' So he said, 'Here I am!' And he said, 'Do not lay your hand on the lad, or do anything to him; for now I know that you fear God, since you have not withheld your son, your only son, from Me. Then Abraham lifted his eyes and looked, and there behind him was a ram caught in a thicket by its horns. So Abraham went and took the ram, and offered it up for a burnt offering instead of his son" (Genesis 22:11–13).

Verses 11–13

The record states that Isaac died . . . "By faith Abraham, when he was tried, OFFERED UP Isaac; and he that had received the promises OFFERED UP his ONLY BEGOTTEN SON, . . . "Accounting that God was able to RAISE HIM UP . . . from the DEAD . . . " (Hebrews 11:17&19).

"How long was Isaac dead? Three days . . . exactly three days . . . Abraham actually offered up his son in the sight of God . . . as far as Abraham was concerned, Isaac was really dead. When Abraham started out on the journey early . . . that morning . . . he had no other idea . . . than that . . . God meant what He said . . . and that he must after three days put Isaac to death on Mt. Moriah. For three days he considered his son, Isaac, dead, potentially dead . . . Isaac had been dead in the mind of Abraham for three days and now all of a sudden he is returned to life."[28]

27. DeHaan, *Adventures in Faith*, 165.
28. DeHaan, *Adventures in Faith*, 166.

What a wonderful picture that after three days Isaac was raised from the dead . . . . Abraham knew the joy of resurrection "upon the (very) mountain where the Son of God was to be slain."[29]

"Abraham believed in the death and the resurrection of his son."[30] Abraham believed the gospel, (the death, burial, and resurrection) and was a child of God. Paul referred to this when he stated,

"And the Scripture, foreseeing that God would justify the Gentiles by faith, preached the gospel to Abraham beforehand, saying, 'In you all nations shall be blessed'" (Galatians 3:8).

The Ram

The ram is a picture of our Lord becoming our substitute, paying the ultimate price for our sins. The ram has played a significant role throughout biblical history. "Its skin provided a mantle for Elijah . . . (it was used to make) the strings of David's harp . . . and its two horns . . . the two trumpets: one to be sounded later at the great revelation of God at Mount Sinai . . . and the other to be blown at . . . the coming of the Messiah (Last Trump)."[31]

"And Abraham called the name of that place Jehovah-Jireh: as it is said to this day, In the mount of the Lord it shall be seen" (Genesis 22:14).

Verse 14

Jehovah-Jireh, the Lord will provide . . . the Lord will see to it. "In the Mount of the Lord, it shall be provided . . . . Should be translated, 'In the mount the Lord shall be seen.'"[32]

"Isaac is a type of the Lord Jesus Christ up to a certain point, and then the ram takes his place and becomes God's provision for the sinner. Abraham understood all the meaning of these things. We hear Jesus saying in John 8:56,

"'Your father Abraham rejoiced to see My day: and he saw it and was glad.'"[33]

29. DeHaan, *Adventures in Faith,* 167.

30. DeHaan, *Adventures in Faith,* 167.

31. Goldstein, *Jewish Legends,* 57–58.

32. Barnhouse, *Genesis,* 204.

33. DeHaan, *Adventures in Faith,* 168–69.

Climbing Your Mountain

Question: Have you climbed a Mount Moriah in your life? Christian, have you been to the mountain of struggling to know God's will? Take comfort in Abraham's faith in the unknown. He did not know exactly how his journey to Mt. Moriah and the sacrifice of Isaac was going to unfold. He only knew that God is true to His Word, that Isaac was the promised child, and that God told him to go to the mountain.

"Often, followers of God wonder how they may know the will of God. Ninety percent of the knowing of the will of God consists in your willingness to do it before it is (completely) known (I and the lad will go up yonder and 'worship'), when we are ready to pick up the knife . . . or . . . to lay it down, God will pour out His richest blessing(s)."[34]

"Faith may be timid when it has not been fully tested . . . and although we are never to trust in previous triumphs . . . but in God alone . . . those triumphs are there as landmarks of the trustworthiness of God."[35]

Look back on your life. Do you see the landmarks? Are you being tested? Are you going through an unbearable trial?

Remember, Jehovah-Jireh, God will provide. He will see to it. God is faithful. Even "if we are faithless, He remains faithful" (2 Timothy 2:13).

Now let me speak to the non-Christian, the seeker, the nonbeliever for a moment. Will you climb the mountain of faith? Believing on the Lord, trusting in Him alone? Will you repent, turning away from sin and turning to the cross? The Scripture states,

"But God demonstrates His own love toward us, in that while we were still sinners, Christ died for us" (Romans 5:8).

This is what this lesson is about. The substitute, the Lamb of God, who takes away our sin when we trust in Him alone. Will you trust Him? Will you come to the foot of the mountain called Mt. Calvary and embrace the cross?

"For God so loved the world that He gave . . . "

He provided. He loves you. Oh, how He loves you.

---

34. Barnhouse, *Genesis*, 202.
35. Barnhouse, *Genesis*, 203.

———— Chapter 3 ————

The Descent of God

The Ancient Message Exodus 19, 20

IN EXODUS 19 WE have the account of Moses's encounter with God and the receiving of the Torah (Pentateuch or the first five books of the Bible). Almost 2,000 years have passed since God communicated with man in such a direct fashion. The first time was with Adam. Now Moses is chosen to hear, and he will write down, the words of God.

What a responsibility! What a fearful thing to stand before a holy God!

The Revelation of God

One year before, Moses, keeping the flock of Jethro, his father-in-law, led the herd to the backside of the desert and came to Mount Sinai. There he saw a bush on fire, and yet the bush was not consumed. He carefully approached the bush with great curiosity. A marvelous thing happened. God spoke to Moses from the midst of the bush (Exod. 3:4) and told Moses not to come near until he took off his shoes, for he was standing on "holy ground." The Lord told Moses to go back to Egypt and to lead His chosen people, the Jews, out of Egypt and thus out of bondage. God said to Moses, "When thou hast brought forth the people out of Egypt, ye shall serve God upon this mountain" (Exod. 3:12).

Moses went down to Egypt and confronted the Pharaoh. Moses, along with Aaron, "went in and told Pharaoh, Thus saith the Lord God of Israel, Let my people go." The confrontation with Pharaoh, which included the ten plagues and the Passover, unfolded within a year's time.

Moses leads the people out, and they pass through the Red Sea and experience the miracle of God's provision and protection. Now Moses and the tribes of Israel, free from the enslavement and chains of Pharaoh and knowing that God provides and protects, camp before the holy mountain of God.

The Ascent

"And Moses went up unto God" (Exod. 19:3)

How good it was for Moses to go up the mountain. How good it is for man to ascend the mountain of God. It takes courage. It takes commitment, it takes faith, and you must go alone.

"The Lord called unto him out of the mountain"

David writes, "Blessed is the man whom thou choosest and causest to approach unto thee, that he may dwell in thy courts: we shall be satisfied with the goodness of thy house" (Psalm 65:4).

The Descent of God

When you approach God in faith, He will call to you. When you struggle on the rocky cliffs of life's experiences and you look up to the Father of Lights, He will comfort and give you instruction.

"And Moses went up unto God"—As the psalmist wrote, "He bowed the heavens also, and came down . . . He rode upon a cherub, and did fly: yea, he did fly upon the wings of the wind" (Ps. 18:9–10).

Moses ascended, and as the cloud covered the mountain, as the fire and lighting appeared (vss. 9,16–18), and with the thunder, the earth began to quake and the mountain shook. It is said by the ancients, that as the mount quaked, it began to ascend up to God as the Almighty descended upon this lowly planet.

As Moses went up to God, he did not know whether to approach the cloud, to embrace the cloud, or to stand still and bow before God's presence.

The people in the camp trembled (vs. 16) and Moses cried out to God and God answered him (vs. 19). "And the Lord came down upon Mount Sinai, on the top of the mount: and the Lord called Moses up to the top of the mount; and Moses went up" (vs. 20).

Moses had gone only part way up the mount. It wasn't until God called to him to approach the top, to enter the cloud and appear before the very presence of God Himself, that Moses was able to move forward.

You see, man in his own power cannot enter the presence of God. God must let him come in. Man needs help. He needs redemption. He cannot enter heaven in his own strength or power. No matter how good a man may be, he needs God's help. God must open the door. God must open the way.

Moses went inside the cloud "and the sight of the glory of the Lord was like devouring fire on the top of the mount in the eyes of the children of Israel." Moses was in the cloud, in the very presence of God for "forty days and forty nights" (Exod. 24:16–18).

To Flesh and Blood

It amazes me that God chose to give His sacred message to a mortal born of woman. It wasn't to angels the holy words were given. It wasn't to any heavenly host, or to the stars or any other creature. God's message of love, guidance, and redemption was given to man. "What is man, that thou art mindful of him? For thou has made him a little lower than the angels, and has crowned him with glory and honor" (Ps. 8:5–6). The rabbinic sages say that God shrouded Moses with the cloud so that Satan could not find him. In other words, as God was giving Moses His sacred words to record, God was protecting him from the wrath of the evil one.

I marvel that God would give His message to man. God's name is to be honored (Ps. 8:9), and yet, God has magnified His word above his very name (Ps. 138:2) and then gives it to man. "And God spake all these words . . . " (Exod. 20:1).

Amazing!

The Descent of God

Shavuot

The Jews commemorate this encounter with God. The holiday is called *Shavuot*. It is celebrated in May or June, 50 days after the Passover. It is one of the seven feasts described in Leviticus 23. It became known as the day Moses received the Law from Mount Sinai. It is a time that marks Israel's spiritual journey.

This holiday is no small event as Jewish people remember the time God met with a man and gave him a message. The message is found in the first five books of the Bible called the Torah or Pentateuch. These are the books of Moses. He wrote down what God said to him. He wrote down the words that God wanted the people to know.

Pentecost

Pentecost is the Greek of the Hebrew Shavuot. It is the same holiday. However, Christians celebrate Pentecost remembering that, ten days after Messiah's ascension, the Holy Spirit came in His fullness and the Church was born (Acts 2) and thousands came to believe in Jesus.

Jesus rose from the dead on the third day and appeared before many (1 Cor. 15). "For the third day, the Lord will come down in the sight of all the people upon Mount Sinai" (Exod. 19:11). When Jesus died on the cross the curtain in the temple that separated the people from the Holy of Holies was torn in two. This opened the entrance to the place where the cloud, the shekinah, the glory or presence of God appeared.

On this day, common bread was eaten. Not the special bread of the other holidays. The common man could easily participate in the celebration. When the curtain was torn and the place was opened up, it was exposed to all who would pass by the temple. The main doors were opened, and everyone could see directly into the most sacred place of all.

Pentecost is a celebration of the birth of the church. It commemorates the fact that all believers are indwelt by the Holy Spirit. Because they are indwelt by the Holy Spirit, they have access to God directly. They can enter His presence through relationship and faith. The common man, not only a high priest, can approach God through His Word and Spirit. The curtain was torn, the veil removed, and all who come through the cross and believe can enter a personal relationship with God in Christ.

The Christian Meaning

1. Respect the Holy—God told Moses to take off his shoes for he was standing on holy ground (Exod. 3:5). In a world where little reverence is expressed for things of God, we are reminded in this account to pause and value that which is from the Holy One.

   On the south side of the temple, we find that the steps leading up to this sacred place are designed in a certain way. You have one wide step and then one narrow step. You must pause and pay attention while you ascend. If not, you may stumble climbing the steps. That was the idea—to pause, and reflect; to realize, that where you were ascending was a holy place that needed respect and reverence.

The Bible, baptism, communion, preaching and teaching of the Scripture, the place where God's people meet are to name a few things holy that need our respect and reverence.

2. Worship the Holy One—"When you bring forth the people . . . you shall worship God . . . (Exod. 3:12). The Hebrew word *abad* translated "serve" can also be rendered "worship" or "enslaved." Isn't it interesting that God would say something like this, "When you free my people from enslavement in Egypt, I want them to be enslaved to me. Then, they will be truly free." True worship is submission to God. "I and the lad will go yonder and worship" (Gen. 22:5). To be free from your own control, your own desires, your own plan, your own way and letting God have His way in your life is the only way to be truly free.

3. Journey Alone—Each one of us must seek God. You alone must come to terms with God. Moses was in the desert when he found God, or, actually when God approached Moses. Just as Jesus approached and found the disciples and asked them to follow, so it is that God may approach you. However, you alone must respond to Him. Either you believe, or you deny. But you do it alone.

4. God will comfort—"We shall be satisfied with the goodness of thy house" (Psalm 65:4). As we journey through life we will have mountaintop experiences as well as dark valleys of trial and testing. In all of these, we are reminded that God will comfort. As Moses "went up to God," God called to him and gave Moses His precious Word. The Holy Spirit takes these ancient words and brings healing to the soul. The follower of God will come to know the profound comfort of Scripture. "Let my soul live, and it shall praise thee" (Ps. 119:175). Why does my soul live? "Thy word hath quickened me" (Ps. 119:50). In other words, God's Word brings life.

5. To man, God's Word was given—It was to Moses the ancient message was given. God entrusted His message to man. To celebrate this magnificent, mysterious moment in time, the Jews celebrate Shavuot commemorating the giving of the Law to Moses. They decorate their homes and eat special foods with milk and honey products, reminding them of the land of milk and honey. Milk and honey are symbols of

Torah and learning. In the synagogue, the book of Ruth is read during Shavuot. Oftentimes, before reading the Scriptures at home, Jewish families will place a drop of honey on the tongue of each child (even babies). Some will even pour honey on the page of the text and have the child lick the honey off the page. Why? "How sweet are thy words unto my taste! Yea, sweeter than honey to my mouth" (Ps. 119:103). The child associates the learning of Scripture as something sweet.

6. To man, God's Spirit was given—Christians call Shavuot "*Pentecost*." There was thunder and lightning, a thick cloud, and a sound of a trumpet (shofar) when Moses ascended the mountain. Pentecost was also a day marked by unique events. "A sound from heaven as of a rushing mighty wind . . . There appeared cloven tongues like as of fire" (Acts 2:2–3).

   Just like the eerie sound of the trumpet on Mount Sinai, the wind blew on Mount Zion. And, just like the thunder and lightning appeared on Mount Sinai, the cloven fire appeared on Mount Zion. On this day, the followers of Moses received the Law on Mount Sinai. On this day, 1,500 years later, the followers of Jesus, the Messiah, received the Holy Spirit and the birth of the Church on Mount Zion. [/NL 1-6]

The Shofar

A side note here: The first reference of the shofar (ram's horn) in Scripture is found when Moses went up to God. The shofar was also used to announce the beginning of the Shabbat. Joshua used the shofar to bring the walls down. All throughout the Tanakh (Old Testament), you will find references to the shofar. Some say that it was Abraham who blew the shofar for the first time to worship God in providing the ram in Genesis 22.

It is interesting to note that the blowing of the shofar is associated with the return of Messiah and the rapture of the Church (Matt. 24:31; 1 Cor. 15:52; 1 Thess. 4:16). The Jewish Tanakh ends with 2 Chronicles with a reference of "going up." The B'rit Hadashah (New Covenant; New Testament) ends with "Come up hither" and "even so come, Lord Jesus" (Rev. 4:1; 22:20). Moses went up—the Church will go up.

Begin Your Ascent

God has opened the way for salvation through His Son, Jesus. The gift of salvation has been paid for on the cross. Therefore, eternal life is given to all who believe in Jesus as the Son of God, who is God Himself. However, the journey of sanctification, or spiritual growth and maturity, is a difficult journey. It is, as it were, a journey up the mountain. Nevertheless, each Christian must decide to ascend. God will not force you to climb. If you begin to climb, the cost will be great and the path difficult.

God will be with you each step of the way. He will call out to you through His Word and Spirit. He will protect you from the evil one. If you decide to climb, you will never be the same. Like Moses, it will take courage, it will take commitment, it will take faith, and you must go alone. But it will be worth it!

Begin your ascent now and trust God.

> *"Fear not: for I have redeemed thee, I have called thee*
> *by thy name; thou art mine.*
> *When thou passest through the waters, I will be with thee;*
> *and through the rivers, they shall not overflow thee:*
> *when thou walkest through the fire, thou shalt not be burned;*
> *neither shall the flame kindle upon thee, for I am the Lord thy God,*
> *the Holy One of Israel, thy Savior"* (Isa. 43:1–3).

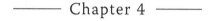

Chapter 4

Behold, His Yeshua!

Psalm 91

FOR LOUISE, MY ANCHOR of true faith and courage, and a true woman of God.

Prayer for Health

By Rabbi Chaim Yosef David Azulai (1724–1806)

Master of the Universe: With Your compassion, grant us the physical strength, health, and ability so that we may function effectively, and may we experience no illness or pain. Enable us to serve You in joy, contentment, and health. Save us from all evil and prolong our days in goodness and our years in sweetness. Enrich our years and add to our days and years of dedicated service to You. Shield us in the shadow of Your wings and spare us and all our family from all harsh or evil decrees. May we be at rest and calm, vigorous, and fresh to serve and revere You.

Foreword

Throughout the ages, the Psalms have been the worship book of both church and synagogue. The prayers and songs recorded there teach us much about the character of God and how to approach Him. From them, we also experience solace in time of trouble and are inspired to praise our Creator.

Few psalms, however, are as beloved as Psalm 91. Through it, we are reminded of the amazing truth that when we make the Almighty our dwelling place, whatever trials may come, we are protected, and we do not face them alone. We can also rest assured that God's purposes will always be fulfilled even in (or despite) the snares and strategies of the evil one. The cultural and Hebrew insights deftly woven throughout this meditation add new depth of understanding; and the prayers of the saints throughout the ages remind us of that great cloud of witnesses who have run the race before. From them, the reader may glean wisdom.

These days, as the world is facing a health and economic crisis, the encouragement found in this devotional is timely, as is the challenge toward increased trust and intimacy with our heavenly Father. Through the discipline of prayer and the meditation on the truths in this Psalm highlighted so beautifully by Dr. Johnson, one may indeed find an anchor for the soul.

Nicole Y. Yoder VP Aid and Aliyah, International Christian Embassy Jerusalem; MA Judeo-Christian Synergism, Master's International University of Divinity; MA International Community Development, Northwest University

Preface

Behold, His Yeshua! was written during the beginning of the pandemic of 2019–20. This pandemic and its disease brought about great fear and despair.

Over a period of several weeks, this nine-part series was emailed to Israel Today Ministries' constituency and put on social media. The response was awe-inspiring. Requests came for a booklet to become available. Here it is. No claim is made for originality, but the writer is deeply grateful for the help he received from many sources, including those in the bibliography found at the end of this chapter.

May your heart be strengthened, full of peace, and have great certainty about God's protection as you reflect upon the words of this profound psalm.

Part One: No Need to Fear (Ps. 91:1)

"He who dwells in the shelter of the Most High will abide in the shadow of the Almighty" (v. 1).

Psalm 91 speaks of God's protection from dangers and things like plagues. The Talmud refers to Psalm 91 as *The Song of Plagues* (Shev Shema'tata

15b). This psalm might have been sung by two people antiphonally—there is a *profound paused ending* where God speaks in verses 14–16.

This psalm is read in the synagogue on Saturday mornings and at the close of the evening services on Saturday night and at funeral services. I personally end my official letters and notes with my signature and Psalm 91.

Traditional Jewish thought is that Moses wrote Psalm 91 during the wilderness wanderings and that David compiled the psalm and added it to his book of psalms. Whether the author is Moses or David, the psalm is profound.

The psalm is wonderful to meditate upon and to pray back to God.

"He who dwells in the shelter (Hebrew: *sayther*—cover) of the Most High *(Elyon)* will abide in the shadow (Hebrew: *tsale*—shade) of the Almighty *(Shaddai)*" (v. 1).

Shelter. . .shade literally means "secret hiding place." Believers feel protected from pursuing enemies (Ps. 31:20–21). This protectiveness comes from the reality found in Genesis 19:8 where the "men" found "shelter or shade" in Lot's home from the pursuing enemies. Even today, with Bedouins, and generally throughout the Middle East, those who enter their homes come under their "shade" or protection. The idea of great hospitality, protection, and provision comes from the Hebrew word *Hesed* often translated "mercy."

Shaddai and *Elyon* are ancient names of God. God revealed the name *Shaddai* (Almighty) to Abraham (Exod. 6:3) before He revealed His unspeakable name of *YHVH* (Exod. 3:14; 15:3). Rather than attempting to pronounce *YHVH*, as many Christians do, Jews will say, *Adonai* or *HaShem*.

Points to Ponder

1. Believers are in the "shade" of the Almighty.

2. We are protected from harm and from anything or anyone pursuing us.

3. God will never abandon His children.

4. There is no need to fear; He will help us (Heb. 13:5– 6; Isa. 41:13).

Read and meditate upon the verses mentioned in this brief devotional. When tempted to fear, remember what God said in verse one, and like a child, reach up and take hold of His hand and feel safe in His "shade" and protection.

PRAYER

We beseech thee, Master, to be our helper and protector.
Save the afflicted among us; have mercy on the lowly;
Raise up the fallen; appear to the needy; heal the ungodly;
Restore the wanderers of thy people;
Feed the hungry; ransom our prisoners;
Raise up the sick; comfort the faint-hearted.

—Clement of Rome (1st Century)

Part Two: You are the Temple! (Ps. 91:2–4)

*"I will say to the Lord (Adonai), 'My refuge and my fortress,
My God (Elohi[m]), in whom I trust'" (v. 2).*

Refuge and *fortress* are very strong expressions indicating that God is sovereign, the ruler of the universe.

Shelter of the Most High (v. 1) and *refuge, fortress* (v. 2) are references to the Temple where the presence of God dwelt. As dangers from demons, war, wild beasts, and plagues do exist and do happen to believers, protection, security, and peace were found within the Temple. "For in the day of trouble He will conceal me in His tabernacle; In the secret place of His tent He will hide me; He will lift me up on a rock" (Ps. 27:5).

Within the psalm there is an interchange of first and second persons (first person: I/We; second person: You). God directly speaks in verses 14–16.

"For it is He who delivers you from the snare of the trapper and from the deadly pestilence" (v. 3).

The second person speaks. *Trapper* refers to the fowler, the one who entraps birds. The implication is that God will protect you from the dangerous attempts against your life that comes from evil, pestilence, famine, et.al.

"He will cover you with His pinions, and under His wings you may seek refuge; His faithfulness is a shield and bulwark" (v.4).

This is the verse I use when I sign letters and correspondence, I write:

Shalom and Blessings,
Until He comes, we are
Together Under His Wings,

Pinions is a reference to a bird spreading its wings over its young in the nest protecting, shielding, covering, hiding them from potential danger.

Under His wings according to Rashi (1040–1105) is the Shekinah (Divine Presence of God). Believers rest in His shadow, for God protects them. The wings may also refer to the cherubim on either side of the Ark (Exod. 25:17–22). The Divine Presence hovered over the Ark.

Shield: A shield could in fact completely surround and protect the warrior. The Talmud suggests it was a shield that moved round about him (Ibn Ezra and Targum).

Bulwark: A bulwark is a wall, a barricade, protection, and defense against attack.

Both shield and bulwark are an encompassing shield of protection.

Points to Ponder

1. God is sovereign, the ruler of the universe.

2. Believers are under the Divine Presence of God.

3. God's protection is an encompassing shield.

4. The Temple, where the presence of God dwells, is where you find safety and peace.

5. For those of you who are believers in Jesus remember Paul's words: *"Your body is the temple of the Holy Spirit who is in you, whom you have from God, and you are not your own? For you were bought at a price; therefore, glorify God in your body and in your spirit, which are God's"* (1 Cor. 6:19–20 [NKJV]).

6. The peace, protection, and safety we all long for is found in Jesus. The presence of God, through the Holy Spirit, dwells in you. We need not fear.

". . .In the world, you will have tribulation; but be of good cheer, I have overcome the world" (John 16:33 (NKJV)).

"Peace I leave with you, My peace I give to you; not as the world gives do I give to you. Let not your heart be troubled, neither let it be afraid" (John 14:27 (NKJV)).

Prayer

Lord, because you have made me, I owe you the whole of my love;

because you have redeemed me, I owe you the whole of myself;

because you have promised so much, I owe you my whole being.

Moreover, I owe you as much more love than myself as you are greater than I,

for whom you gave yourself and to whom you promised yourself.

I pray you, Lord, make me taste by love what I taste by knowledge;

let me know by love what I know by understanding.

I owe you more than my whole self, but I have no more,

and by myself I cannot render the whole of it to you.

Draw me to you, Lord, in the fullness of your love.

I am wholly yours by creation; make me all yours, too, in love.

—Anselm (AD 1033–1109)

Part Three: Deadly Sandstorms: What Happens in the Darkness? (Ps. 91:5–6)

"You will not be afraid of the terror by night, or of the arrow that flies by day; of the pestilence that stalks in darkness, or of the destruction that lays waste at noon" (vv. 5–6).

Terror by night is the absence of light. In the light, you can see and understand. However, in the darkness, just as today, ancient folklore told of demons and evil spirits who lurked in the opaque atmosphere of night. When you are alone at night, not knowing who or what is out there, you need not fear, for God will protect your soul and your being.

Arrow that flies by day is not a human weapon, rather, metaphorically some demonic power. "The Lord will protect you from all evil: He will keep your soul. The Lord will guard your going out and your coming in from this time forth and forever" (Ps. 121:7–8; cf. Song 3:8).

Pestilence: The context is that of demons or envoys of evil.

Destruction: The Hebrew word is *qetev* meaning "destroying, to cut-off, to scourge" like that of a scorching desert wind or a deadly sandstorm.

Points to Ponder

1. God protects in the darkness, where there is no light, and at noon, when the brightest of the light shines.

2. Jesus taught his disciples, "What I tell you in the darkness, speak in the light; and what you hear whispered in your ear, proclaim upon the housetops" (Matt. 10:27).

3. It is in the darkness that we learn to listen to Jesus. It is during the times of trial and uncertain circumstances that He whispers in our ears.

4. To hear Him, we must be quiet. If we talk or move around busying ourselves with "helps," we may not hear. Be silent and pause.

5. Listen to what God wants to say through the Holy Spirit, and then, in the light, shout it from the rooftops or simply share with your neighbor or loved one.

6. Through the discipline, we learn that in the darkness humility comes and our hearts grow into clay from stone, and then we can hear God.

Prayer

Lord, thou hast given us thy Word for a light to shine upon our path; grant us so to meditate on that Word, and to follow its teaching, that we may find in it the light that shines more and more until the perfect day, through Jesus Christ our Lord.

—Jerome (ca. AD 342–420)

Part Four: Come, and See! (Ps. 91:7–8)

"A thousand may fall at your side and ten thousand at your right hand, but it shall not approach you. You will only look on with your eyes and see the recompense of the wicked" (vv.7–8).

At your side is referencing the left side, as compared to the right (hand) side. It is a Hebraic poetic nuance. The right hand emphasizes strength.

It is referring to the "arrow" in verse 5, the pestilence, the envoys of evil and destruction.

Shall not approach you comforts us in knowing that we who believe and trust in God will be secure. Multitudes who do not have God's protection, because of their unbelief, will fall around us. However, believers need not worry.

Your eyes. . .see: Because no harm comes to the believer, they will see the wicked defeated with their very own eyes. With their own eyes, they will see God's power.

Jesus said, "Come, and . . . see" (John 1:39). Andrew said to Simon, "We have found the Messiah" (John 1:41). To "come" is an act of faith. Faith opens one's eyes to see the Messiah.

The enemy attacks us all. "When the devil had finished every temptation, he left Him until an opportune time" (Luke 4:13). Satan tempted Jesus for forty days in the wilderness, but Jesus defeated Satan by quoting Scripture. Satan left Him for a season "until an opportune time," which was during the agony of Gethsemane.

"Then He said to them, 'My soul is deeply grieved, to the point of death; remain here and keep watch with Me.' And He went a little beyond them, and fell on His face and prayed, saying, 'My Father, if it is possible, let this cup pass from Me; yet not as I will, but as You will.'. . .He went away again a second time and prayed, saying, 'My Father, if this cannot pass away unless I drink it, Your will be done.'. . .And He left them again, and went away and prayed a third time, saying the same thing once more." (Matt. 26:38–39, 42, and 44).

Satan's final onslaught against Jesus as the "Son of Man" was at Gethsemane. "Son of Man" is a messianic term which implies His humanity, in contrast to the term "Son of God" which implies His divinity. Jesus was both fully "human" and fully "God."

The *cup* refers to His approaching death (Matt. 20:22). His humanity struggled and was tested in the garden. He was about to taste the pungent filth in the cup of death for the sin of the world.

If this cup may not pass away. . .thy will be done is a Greek nuance that something is determined as fulfilled, that, it is *true*. The Son of Man acquiesced to the Father's will fulfilling His destiny as the Son of God who became the Passover lamb, the Savior of the world. He made it possible for sinners to become sons (Greek: *tekna*—children) of God. His agony, His test, His moment of surrender was the beginning of our salvation. The crucifixion was the victory of the Son of Man over Satan's test.

His submission at Gethsemane surrendering to the fact that He was to die and become the "Sin Offering," the sacrifice, to save humanity from sin, changed humanity's compass forever. *Gethsemane* means "oil press" indicating the Son of Man was pressed into submission ("His sweat became like drops of blood" (Luke 22:44)) to the will of the Father. As a result, every person can now enter the presence of God because of what the Son of Man did. Through Jesus, anyone can "Come, and . . . see."

Points to Ponder

1. Satan attacks us all. Jesus was attacked.

2. The Lord prayed three times before complete surrender to the Father's will. Paul prayed three times to the Lord about a "thorn in the flesh." God said no, that His grace was sufficient (2 Cor. 12:7–10). There were two attempts to heal the blind man at Bethsaida (Mark 8:22–25). When the trials come, believers pray. Sometimes the answer comes swiftly, and at times slowly, but an answer will come—either yes or no.

3. Jesus has made it possible for our redemption and peace.

4. We are not victims; we are conquerors.

5. People who haven't learned how to love often have a victim's mentality.

6. People who love do not feel limited. "Because he has loved Me, therefore I will deliver him" (Ps. 91:14).

Prayer

O Lord, who hast mercy upon all, take away from me my sins,
and mercifully kindle in me the fire of thy Holy Spirit.
Take away from me the heart of stone, and give me a heart of
flesh,
a heart to love and adore thee,
a heart to delight in thee,
to follow and to enjoy thee, for Christ's sake.

—Ambrose of Milan (ca. AD 339–397)

Part Five: Haven of Rest (Ps. 91:9–10)

"For you have made the Lord, my refuge, even the Most High, your dwelling place. No evil will befall you, nor will any plague come near your tent" (vv. 9–10).

Refuge is the Hebrew word *"makseh"* which means refuge, or shelter from the storm, from danger of falsehood. Another word translated "refuge" is found in Psalm

16:1—"Preserve me, O God, for I take refuge in You." This Hebrew word is *Chasithi* (Ka-see-tee) meaning "to seek refuge, to flee for protection, to put trust and hope in God." In Psalm 16, David was crying out to God for protection to guard him from evil. David was a man after God's own heart (1 Sam. 13:14; Acts 13:22). David's heart was joined with God's. David made many mistakes, from adultery to murder, and he knew that the enemy sought after his soul endeavoring to cause him to sin. He was saying that "I will put my trust in your protection, and I will put my trust in your truth—your Word is truth."

Sometimes we do things being misguided by our thoughts and our self-perceived spirituality. We justify things in our heart, only to find out later that we made the wrong choice and the ramifications were severe. David knew this experience and was reaching out to God for help. He did not want to wander from God's path.

". . .Even the Most High, your dwelling place. No evil will befall you, nor will any plague come near your tent."

The LXX (Septuagint: Greek Old Testament—Jews used this version principally at the time of Jesus) translates verses nine and ten this way, "For thou, O Lord, art my hope: Thou my soul, hast made the Most High thy refuge. No evils shall come upon thee, and no scourge shall draw nigh to thy dwelling."

The emphasis is a little clearer in the LXX. God's dwelling is on high— the "Most High" (Hebrew: *Elyon*)— and is out of reach for those "evils" pursuing you. God's protection is a "haven of rest." He is truly our "refuge" in troubled times.

Points to Ponder

1. God does not keep us free from trouble.

2. When trouble comes, He gives us choices to make. The psalmist chose to make the "Most High" his refuge. We have a choice to run toward or run away from God during times of trial.

3. Our plans, our schemes, our strengths, and our failures are some of the things that seemingly would put a wedge between us and God.

4. Nothing can separate us from His love (Rom. 8:35–39).

5. Like David, we always can reach out to God who loves us and seek refuge in His haven, so that we do not wander away from His path.

6. Life without hardships and testing is impossible, whether in the flesh or the spirit.

7. God has given each of us free will. We choose.

8. Virtue, strength, and wisdom physically and spiritually are acquired.

9. We must discipline both body and spirit.

10. Resistance, testing, and difficulty strengthen both the body and the spirit. And all of us will experience these difficulties. When the enemy comes, remember the words of our Master: "These things I have spoken unto you, that in me ye might have peace. In the world ye shall have tribulation: but be of good cheer; I have overcome the world" (John 16:33).

11. Holiness, security, and peace unfolds as we trust in the protection and truth of the "Most High."

Prayer

We ask you, Master, be our helper and defender. Rescue those of our number in distress; raise up the fallen; assist the needy; heal the sick; turn back those of your people who stray; feed the hungry; release our captives; revive the weak; encourage those who lose heart. Let all the nations realize that you are the only God, that Jesus Christ is your Child, and that we are your people and the sheep of your pasture.

—First Epistle of Clement (ca. AD 96)

Part Six: Face to Face with God and Angels (Ps. 91:11)

"For He will give His angels charge concerning you, to guard you in all your ways" (v. 11).

Angels are like divine bodyguards. *Angel* (Hebrew: *malach*) means a "messenger" who communicates the king's wishes. An angel represents the king—God, the king. God sends angels to fulfill a specific task, a mission of God's choosing. The Talmud says that certain angels accompany a person throughout their life (Chagigah 16a). The Talmud is correct.

"Are they not all ministering spirits, sent out to render service for the sake of those who will inherit salvation?" (Heb. 1:14) This gives voice to the fact that angels not only serve Jesus (Matt. 4:11), but they also serve His children or "those who will inherit salvation."

"See that you do not despise one of these little ones, for I say to you that their angels in heaven continually see the face of My Father who is in heaven" (Matt. 18:10).

Face: In Exodus 33:11, it is said that the Lord spoke with Moses face-to-face (Hebrew: *p'anim al p'anim*). Face to face is a very intimate position. When God spoke to Moses "face-to-face," it was a very intimate and otherworldly moment. In Matthew 18:10, Jesus warns those who would harm children and implies that judgment would be severe upon those who abuse. The angels assigned to little ones have intimate conversations with God face-to-face. He knows who harms the children.

Guard you in all your ways refers to protection from the evil onslaught of influences and attacks against God's people. *Ways* is the Hebrew word *derek* meaning one's journey, manner of one's course of life, or moral character, one's walk.

As evil attempts to persuade and dissuade our choices and our actions, angels will guard us as we walk. These divine bodyguards are protecting us from evil attack. In Daniel 10, the angel sent to Daniel with an answer was in battle with a satanic adversary. Michael, the prince of angels who watches over Israel (Dan. 12:1), came and helped defeat the adversary. Meanwhile, Daniel wrestled in prayer with no answer for twenty-one days. Though perhaps uncertain and tired, he kept "walking" in moral character and faith. The answer did come.

God Himself is sometimes camouflaged as an angel. "Now the Lord (YHVH) appeared to him by the [terebinths] of Mamre, while he was sitting at the tent door in the heat of the day. When he lifted up his eyes and looked, behold, three men were standing opposite him; and when he saw them, he ran from the tent door to meet them and bowed himself to the earth, and said, 'My Lord (*Adonai*), if now I have found favor in your sight, please do not pass your servant by'" (Gen. 18:1–3).

Abraham was sitting at the tent door in the heat of the day when three men appeared before him. Rabbinic scholars attest that he was still recovering from his circumcision (Gen. 17:24). Immediately, he recognized that one of the three was the Lord and the other two angels. Though in discomfort from the circumcision, he ran toward them and bowed before them, his face pressed in the earth. He washed their feet and brought food and drink, and he stood off to the side while they were eating. He knew who they were. After the meal, one of the angels said that Sarah would become pregnant and bear a son. She laughed. And the Lord asked, "Is anything too difficult for the Lord?" (Gen. 18:14) Or is anything too "marvelous for the Lord?"

Points to Ponder

1. Our divine bodyguards (angels) fight for us.

2. Our angels have intimate conversations with God.

3. As we journey with God and trials come, even when we do not have immediate answers, we must persevere and keep walking until the answer comes.

4. Develop a sense of awe, reverence, and expectancy for the Lord's presence. There is no pretentiousness here, no artificial posturing. A developed sense of spiritual intuition acknowledges the Lord is in our midst.

5. Abraham's acts of humility, reverence, washing feet, and serving them is a mirror of what Jesus taught His disciples (John 13; Matt. 20:28). In times of trial or healing through pain, we are to serve and worship God—it's not about us; it's about Him.

6. As with Sarah, God knows our heart and how we often teeter questioning what He says. When pushed, we deny that we "laughed." Fear of the unknown often causes us to recoil. But then, low and behold, the miraculous happens.

7. God can do the impossible!

Prayer

When you are alone, you should know that there is present with you the angel whom God has appointed for each man. . . . This angel, who is sleepless and cannot be deceived, is always present with you; he sees all things and is not hindered by darkness. You should know, too, that with him is God, who is in every place; for there is no place and nothing material in which God is not, since He is greater than all things and holds all men in His hand.

—St. Anthony the Great (Anthony of Egypt, AD 251–356).

Part Seven: Anxiety Fades; Satan Broken (Ps. 91:12–13)

"They will bear you up in their hands, that you do not strike your foot against a stone. You will tread upon the lion and cobra, the young lion and the serpent you will trample down" (vv. 12–13).

Your foot against a stone: The context of the psalm emphasizes that angels carry us up in their hands and, as a result, we journey differently. The usual human troubles that come in life are faded, and we are spared.

Lion and cobra represent dangerous enemies, both physical and spiritual. The psalmist will overcome as angels protect him from the complexities and anxiety of the attack.

Both rabbinical and evangelical scholars submit that guardian angels protect God's people (Exod. 23:20; Psalm 34:7; 103:20; Matt. 18:10; Heb. 1:14). "Bless the Lord, you His angels, mighty in strength, who perform His word, obeying the voice of His word" (Psalm 103:20).

These two verses (Ps. 91:12–13) direct us to something, or should I say, to someone greater.

"And he led Him to Jerusalem and had Him stand on the pinnacle of the temple, and said to Him, 'If You are the Son of God, throw yourself down from here; for it is written, He will command His angels concerning You to guard You, and on their hands they will bear You up, so that You will not strike Your foot against a stone.' And Jesus answered and said to him, 'It is said, You shall not put the Lord Your God to the test.' When the devil had finished every temptation, he left Him" (Luke 4:9–13; cf. Matt. 4).

Satan uses the same temptations he used with Adam and Eve.

1. *Temptation of the flesh*: You may eat of any tree (Gen. 3:1); If you are the Son of God, tell this stone to become bread (Luke 4:3).

2. *Temptation of private gain:* You will not die (Gen. 3:4); You will not hurt Your foot (Luke 4:11).

3. *Temptation of personal power:* You will be like God (Gen. 3:5); I will give you all this (Luke 4:5–6).

All temptations are wrapped up in these three points.

Had Jesus acquiesced to Satan's temptations He would have been yielding to a lesser power and would have nullified Himself as Messiah and Savior of the world.

Jesus highlights Psalm 91:13 to His disciples.

"The seventy returned with joy, saying, 'Lord, even the demons are subject to us in Your name.' And He said to them, 'I was watching Satan fall from heaven like lightning. Behold, I have given you authority to tread on serpents and scorpions, and over all power of the enemy, and nothing will injure you. Nevertheless, do not rejoice in this, that the spirits are subject to you, but rejoice that your names are recorded in heaven'" (Luke 10: 17–20).

The disciples were elated they were victorious in their service to the Master. Jesus responded saying, "I was watching Satan fall from heaven like lightning." This does not mean that at that moment Satan was falling from heaven. Satan wishes he had the power of heaven (Isaiah 14:12–17), but he does not! Jesus was saying that Satan was falling from greatness and his dominion. His power had been broken, and in the name of Jesus, Satan was brought to his knees, bowing before the authority of God the Son.

Points to Ponder

1. Our walk is different as angels carry us in their hands.

2. Anxiety fades and complications diminish from the enemies' attacks because angels perform God's Word on our behalf.

3. Satan is brought to his knees before the authority of the name of Jesus.

4. We rejoice, not because of the deeds we do in service of the Lord, but rather we rejoice in the work that God does through us. It is all Him, not anything that we do; therefore, we boast in Him and humbly praise Him that our "names are recorded in heaven."

Prayer

Let us think of the whole host of angels, how they stand by and serve his will, for Scriptures say: "Ten thousand times ten thousand were doing service to him, and they cried out: Holy, holy, holy, Lord Sabaoth; the whole of creation is full of His glory." Then let us gather together in awareness of our concord, as with one mouth we shout earnestly to him that we may become sharers in his great and glorious promises.

—Clement of Rome (ca. AD 96)

Part Eight: You Know My Name! (Ps. 91:14)

"Because he has loved Me, therefore I will deliver him; I will set him securely on high, because he has known My name" (v.14).

Within the initial part of the psalm, there is a tradeoff discussion between first and second persons (first person: I/We; second person: You). The Targum, an Aramaic paraphrase and interpretation of the Hebrew Bible of the first century, suggests that the dialogue is between David and Solomon. Now in verses 14–16, God directly speaks.

Because he has loved Me: When someone loves another, self is completely diminished (Matt. 16:24), and one's sole purpose is to attempt to please the one loved. There is a willingness to sacrifice heart, mind, and soul for the one you love. We love God because He first loved us (1 John 4:19).

God, speaking in the first person, responds to the psalmist, "Because he has loved Me, I will deliver him." This means God will protect, rescue, and be with him in times of peril and trouble, protecting him from harm as revealed in verses one and four as he abides in the *shade* under the wings of the Almighty. It is a sense of "honor" that God bestows upon the one who loves Him.

On high is a haven, as in verse nine, which is a place that God puts the one who loves Him. It is a place where God dwells and is out of the reach of the "evils" pursuing him.

Known my name: The Hebrew word *yada* means "to know"—an intimacy, a closeness to God, having a longing for, or devotion to God.

In Exodus 3:13–15, Moses asked God, "What is your name?"

God stated, "*Ehyeh Asher Ehyeh*—I am who I am—I am the be-ing. . .The Lord *(YHVH)*. . .this is My name forever, and thus I am to be remembered throughout all generations."

God names himself as the God who is, who was, and will be. In dis-closing His name, God is revealing His mercy to His people.

Ehyeh (I Am) can also be translated "I will be what I will be." Simply, yet profoundly, God is always totally "I Am" or "I am the One who is." This is His name forever, and this is His title for all generations. God is saying you may call me by my name, but don't ever think you can fully compre-hend me. "I am that I am. I exist; I will be who I will be."

God is God. He does not need us to confirm He exists—He profoundly "IS." He created us and then included us, offering us His Name. He reveals Himself to us. He lets Himself be known. "I have manifested Your name to the men whom You gave Me out of the world; they were Yours and You gave them to Me, and they have kept Your word. . . . I have made Your name known to them, and will make it known, so that the love with which You loved Me may be in them, and I in them" (John 17:6, 26).

Points to Ponder

1. The one who loves God will be protected from harm as he abides in God's shade under His wings.

2. The one who loves God knows His name, implying intimacy and an abandonment of will, like a slave. Paul said he was a slave to Christ in which every part of his being belongs to God (Rom. 1:1; 2 Cor. 10:5).

May God bless us as we abide in God's shade, protected under His wings! Encourage one another during challenging times. Pray for one another, and bless your family and neighbor. We are "salt and light" in a world full of fear. Give them hope. The Gospel is hope.

Prayer

Lord Jesus Christ, Keeper and Preserver of all things, let Thy right hand guard us by day and by night, when we sit at home, and when we walk abroad, when we lie down and when we rise up, that we may be kept from all evil, and have mercy upon us sinners. Amen.

— Nerses of Clajes (AD 335–373)

Part Nine: Behold, His Yeshua! (Ps. 91:15–16)

"He will call upon Me, and I will answer him; I will be with him in trouble; I will rescue him and honor him. With a long life, I will satisfy him and let him see My salvation" (vv.15–16).

I will answer him: Religious Jews pray three times a day—morning, afternoon, and evening. These times were model by the patriarchs: Abraham prayed in the morning, Genesis 19:27; Isaac prayed in the afternoon, Genesis 24:63; Jacob prayed at night, Genesis 32:9–22. God heard the psalmist prayers and answered Him.

I will be with him in trouble; I will rescue him: God is reassuring him that he will be protected from the enemy of physical or spiritual harm. God is reminding the psalmist that He will hold his hand and that He will help, saying "Do not fear" and I got you! (Isa. 41:13; cf. John 14:27).

And honor him: God will take away his troubles, and his neighbors will honor him as he was victorious over his enemies. His status in the community has now changed as he acknowledges it was God who brought the victory.

Long life: Psalm 90:10 reminds us of the shortness of life. However, sometimes, God gives us a long life with favor and satisfaction.

Satisfy comes from the Hebrew root *saba* or *sava* which means to be satisfied fully, continually. It is also the word used for grandfather—*saba*. A long life often brings the blessing of children and children's children. A grandparent is satisfied fully, indeed.

See My salvation: Our word "salvation" is *Yeshua* in the Hebrew. *Yeshua* is the Hebrew word for Jesus. Those who love God will see His *Yeshua*. Jesus said, "He who has seen Me has seen the Father" (John 14:9). Those who love God will behold Jesus. To love God is to love Jesus, for Jesus is God (John 1:1, 14).

Points to Ponder

1. Why do Jews pray three times a day?

    a. Blessings come when the sun rises; therefore, we praise Him (Lam. 3:22–24; Ps. 90:14).

b. In the afternoon, as the sun begins to go down, we become concerned, we worry, and we begin to fear, so we pray (Ps. 94:19; 118:6).

c. At night, in the complete darkness, danger lurks, and we cry out to God (Ps. 34:17–19).

2. Our days are numbered (Ps. 90:10, 12). Whether we have a long life or a short life, for those who love God, our eyes behold His *Yeshua* (Jesus, Salvation); therefore, day by day and moment by moment, in the blessings and during trials, we will see Jesus!

May our eyes be full of Jesus during days of testing!

Prayer

In the evening and morning and noonday we praise Thee, we thank Thee, and pray Thee, Master of all, to direct our prayers as incense before Thee. Let not our hearts turn away to words or thoughts of wickedness, but keep us from all things that might hurt us; for to Thee, O Lord, our eyes look up, and our hope is in Thee: confound us not, O our God; for the sake of Jesus Christ our Lord. Amen.

—Eastern Church Vespers

Our Father and our God, we pray that in this period of crisis in our world that the Holy Spirit will use it to remind us of our need of Thee and our relationship with Thee and we pray that tonight if our relationship is not right that we'll make it right through Jesus Christ our Lord who came to die on the cross because He loved us. For we ask it in His Name. Amen.

—Billy Graham (Sacramento, California 1983)

Chapter Endorsements

One hundred and twelve. That is how many Hebrew words comprise Psalm 91. How can a mere one hundred and twelve words be so profound, timeless, and life changing? The Sages of Israel state that spiritual greatness is found in the physically small, and Dr. Johnson has proven this true with this handful of pages. This small chapter about this short psalm will open a sublime and limitless world of truth and insight. "Behold His Yeshua" allows us to look through the keyhole of Psalm 91 and behold wonders.

—L. Grant Luton, Congregational Leader, Beth Tikkun Messianic Congregation, Uniontown, Ohio

Well written and overflowing with hope, encouragement and security for God's people. A must read.

—Richard Donofrio, Senior Pastor, Faith Bible Church, Agawam, Massachusetts

Dr. Johnson weaves the Hebrew text throughout his insights to create a beautiful tapestry of Adonai's love and protection. As you meditate on the truth that is revealed, your thoughts will be transformed, from the mundane to the profound. Your soul and spirit will be lifted high above the heavens, and your appreciation for Elohim (the living God) will forever change your paradigm of the eternal.

—Robert R. Horger, President/ CEO, United Surface Finishing, Inc., Canton, Ohio

— Chapter 5 —

The Arrival

Luke Chapters 1 & 2

"A little girl came home from Sunday School triumphantly waving a paper.

'Mommy!' she said. 'My teacher says I drew the most unusual Christmas picture she has ever seen!'

The mother studied the picture for a moment and concluded it was indeed a very peculiar Christmas picture. 'This is wonderfully drawn, but why have you made all these people riding on the back of an airplane?' the mother gently asked.

'It's the flight into Egypt,' the little girl said, with a hint of disappointment that the picture's meaning was not immediately obvious.

'Oh,' the mother said cautiously. 'Well, who is the mean-looking man at the front?'

'That's Pontius, the Pilot,' the girl said, now visibly impatient.

'I see. And here you have Mary and Joseph and the baby,' the mother volunteered. Studying the picture silently for a moment, she summoned the courage to ask, 'But who is this (heavy) man sitting behind Mary?'

The little girl sighed. 'Can't you tell? That's Round John Virgin!'"[1]

We laugh, but indeed, the true meaning of Christmas has been lost in the midst of legend, ignorance, and commercialism. It is easy to forget the purpose and meaning of this most important day.

In eons past, in the eternal mind of God, our loving Lord created the world, the planets, the stars—the universe—so that the pinnacle of His creation, namely man, could understand a little bit of the glory of the

---

1. MacArthur, *God with Us*, 13–14.

Creator. God communed with man in the Garden and after the fall. He communicated with Noah, Abraham, Isaac, and Jacob and then through the prophets, priests, and kings. God communicated a story of an Anointed One who would come—the Messiah of Israel and the world. A Messiah that would become a sacrificial Lamb and ultimately become the Lion of Judah, the King of Kings.

This hope struck a vein deep within the Jewish soul and moved this oppressed and conquered people with a passion of wonder as to when the Anointed One would come. Nearly 400 years have passed since God directly communicated through a prophet. Rome's powerful arm of oppression embraced the known world. And every Jewish girl, since the time of Abraham, wondered if she will be the one chosen through whom Messiah will come. Hope is waning as four centuries have come and gone and no message from God. Until now . . .

Luke 1

"There was in the days of Herod, the king of Judaea, a certain priest named Zacharias, of the course of Abia: and his wife was of the daughters of Aaron, and her name was Elisabeth. And they were both righteous before God, walking in all the commandments and ordinances of the Lord blameless. And they had no child, because that Elisabeth was barren, and they both were now well stricken in years. And it came to pass, that while he executed the priest's office before God in the order of his course, According to the custom of the priest's office, his lot was to burn incense when he went into the temple of the Lord. And the whole multitude of the people were praying without at the time of incense. And there appeared unto him an angel of the Lord standing on the right side of the altar of incense. And when Zacharias saw him, he was troubled, and fear fell upon him. But the angel said unto him, Fear not, Zacharias: for thy prayer is heard; and thy wife Elisabeth shall bear thee a son, and thou shalt call his name John. And thou shalt have joy and gladness; and many shall rejoice at his birth. For he shall be great in the sight of the Lord, and shall drink neither wine nor strong drink; and he shall be filled with the Holy Ghost, even from his mother's womb. And many of the children of Israel shall he turn to the Lord their God. And he shall go before him in the spirit and power of Elias, to turn the hearts of the fathers to the children, and the disobedient to the wisdom of the just; to make ready a people prepared for the Lord. And Zacharias said unto the angel, whereby shall I know this? For I am an old man, and my wife well stricken in years. And the angel answering said unto him, I am Gabriel, that stand in the presence of God; and am sent to speak unto thee, and to shew thee these glad tidings. And, behold, thou shalt be dumb, and not able to speak, until the day that these things shall be performed, because thou believest not my words, which shall be fulfilled in their season. And the people waited for Zacharias, and marvelled that he tarried so long in the temple. And when he came out, he could not speak unto them: and they perceived that he had seen a vision in the temple: for he beckoned unto them, and remained speechless. And it came to pass, that, as soon as the days of his ministration were accomplished, he departed to his own house. And after those days his wife Elisabeth conceived, and hid herself five months, saying, thus hath the Lord dealt with me in the days wherein he looked on me, to take away my reproach among men" (Luke 1:5–25).

John's birth is announced to Zacharias, a priest of the temple. Elizabeth, his wife, will give birth to John the Baptist, who will be the one crying in the wilderness, the one prophesied of old, having the spirit and power of Elijah, preparing the way for the Lord.

Verses 26–38: Messiah's birth announced to Mary.

"And in the sixth month the angel Gabriel was sent from God unto a city of Galilee, named Nazareth, To a virgin espoused to a man whose name was Joseph, of the house of David; and the virgin's name was Mary. And the angel came in unto her, and said, Hail, thou that art highly favoured, the Lord is with thee: blessed art thou among women. And when she saw him, she was troubled at his saying, and cast in her mind what manner of salutation this should be. And the angel said unto her, Fear not, Mary: for thou hast found favour with God. And, behold, thou shalt conceive in thy womb, and bring forth a son, and shalt call his name JESUS. He shall be great, and shall be called the Son of the Highest: and the Lord God shall give unto him the throne of his father David: and he shall reign over the house of Jacob for ever; and of his kingdom there shall be no end. Then said Mary unto the angel, How shall this be, seeing I know not a man? And the angel answered and said unto her, The Holy Ghost shall come upon thee, and the power of the Highest shall overshadow thee: therefore also that holy thing which shall be born of thee shall be called the Son of God. And, behold, thy cousin Elisabeth, she hath also conceived a son in her old age: and this is the sixth month with her, who was called barren. For with God nothing shall be impossible. And Mary said, Behold the handmaid of the Lord; be it unto me according to thy word. And the angel departed from her" (Luke 1:26–38).

Verse 35: The angel's response

The angel's response is a Hebraic expression of "sublime sentiment and poetical style. The angel . . . deals with one of the deepest and holiest mysteries, and for this reason his words are here exalted to a song. In a tender and chaste manner, he declares in the song the fact of the impending pregnancy of the Virgin Mary through divine influence. The Holy Spirit will come upon Mary and overshadow her with His power, through which she will become pregnant.

In the original Greek . . . (the reference is) to the creative operation or power (of the Holy Spirit). The 'power of the Highest' is thus used as synonymous with it. Like a cloud, the symbol of the divine presence in which God appears, the power of the Highest shall overshadow her."[2] " . . . And the spirit of God moved upon the face of the waters" (Gen. 1:2).

> "And Mary arose in those days, and went into the hill country with haste, into a city of Juda; And entered into the house of Zacharias, and saluted Elisabeth. And it came to pass, that, when Elisabeth heard the salutation of Mary, the babe leaped in her womb; and Elisabeth was filled with the Holy Ghost: and she spake out with a loud voice, and said, blessed art thou among women, and blessed is the fruit of thy womb. And whence is this to me, that the mother of my Lord should come to me? For, lo, as soon as the voice of thy salutation sounded in mine ears, the babe leaped in my womb for joy. And blessed is she that believed: for there shall be a performance of those things which were told her from the Lord" (Luke 1:39–45).

Verses 39–45: Mary visits Elizabeth.

"Luke has incorporated in his gospel three complete hymns used by the early Christians: the Magnificat, the Song of Mary (Luke 1:46–55); the Benedictus, the Song of Zacharias (Luke 1:68–79); and Nunc Dimittis,

2. Geldenhuys, *International Commentary*, 76–77.

the Song of Simeon (Luke 2:29–32); each known from the opening words of the Latin Vulgate."[3]

Luke 2

It is written in Haggai that God says, "I will shake heaven and earth, the sea and dry land; and I will shake all nations, and they shall come to the Desire of All Nations . . . " (Hag. 2:6–7).

Verses 1–3

"And it came to pass in those days, that there went out a decree from Caesar Augustus, that all the world should be taxed. (And this taxing was first made when Cyrenius was governor of Syria.) And all went to be taxed, every one into his own city" (Luke 2:1–3).

"In those days"

"Caesar Augustus was the first Roman emperor. His real name was Caius Octavius. He was a great-nephew of Julius Caesar. The word *Augustus* is significant. That was his title. He took the name Caesar by courtesy and by adoption."[4] In time the title Augustus was dropped and the title became Caesar. It was a time of the famous "Pax Romana," so-called Roman Peace. This was a time when the Roman Republic became the Roman Empire and the Romans were under an autocratic ruler. This autocratic ruler and empire "had bludgeoned the world into submission . . . the whole world was crushed under (his) heel."[5]

"Interestingly, a petition for tax relief from the Jews to Caesar Augustus delayed the census for a period of time so that Mary came full term while they were still in Bethlehem."[6]

---

3. Tittle, *Gospel According to Luke*, 5.

4. Morgan, *Gospel According to Luke*, 34.

5. Morgan, *Gospel According to Luke*, 34

6. Rosen, *Y'Shua*, 13

Verses 4–5

"And Joseph also went up from Galilee, out of the city of Nazareth, into Judaea, unto the city of David, which is called Bethlehem; (because he was of the house and lineage of David:) To be taxed with Mary his espoused wife, being great with child" (Luke 2:4–5).

"Joseph, who was of the house of David, had to go to Bethlehem. Here David had been born a thousand years previously. Originally, the town had been called Efratha (Gen. 35:19)."[7] Joseph and Mary, were only two people amid the multitudes that were now in the region. Only two people amid the masses of the Roman Empire. They had no more effect on Caesar Augustus and the Roman Empire than any two of us would have on the president of the United States. Joseph "went up, and Mary traveled with him; two people. Nobody knew about it, except perhaps the friends of Mary and of Joseph and they did not know much about it. But look again. Two individuals marching under the orders of Caesar Augustus. Look at the woman. Her womb is the tabernacle of the Son of God as she travels. Look at the man. The one passion of his life is to guard that woman."[8]

The way traveled from Nazareth would have been long and weary, taking at least a three-day journey. They probably came the commonly traveled route along the eastern banks of the Jordan, then through Jericho. This was the warmest part of the country. The journey would have been very difficult. "A sense of rest and peace . . . crept over the travelers when at last they reached the rich fields that surrounded the ancient 'House of Bread', . . . passing through the valley which, like an amphitheater, sweeps up to the (two) heights along which Bethlehem stretches, ascending through the terraced vineyards and gardens."[9] Perhaps they recalled the stories of Ruth and Boaz, Jesse and David.

"That edict of Caesar Augustus rippled across the world, touching everyone. Even Joseph and Mary must go."[10]

But something greater than this unfolded. A prophecy was written at least 650 years before. In Micah, we read:

"But thou, Bethlehem Ephratah, though thou be little among the thousands of Judah, yet out of thee shall he come forth unto me that is to

---

7. Geldenhuys, *International Commentary*, 100.

8. Morgan, *Gospel According to Luke*, 35.

9. Edersheim, *Life and Times*, 184.

10. Morgan, *Gospel According to Luke*, 35.

be ruler in Israel; whose goings forth have been from of old, from ever-lasting" (Mic. 5:2).

"When I read that, uttered 650 years before these events, I see that the really insignificant person in the drama is the little puppet (in Rome) called Caesar Augustus; and the significant personalities are the woman in whose womb tabernacles the Son of God, and the man who is guarding her."[11]

Luke 2:6–7 reads, "And so it was, that, while they were there, the days were accomplished that she should be delivered. And she brought forth her firstborn son, and wrapped him in swaddling clothes, and laid him in a manger; because there was no room for them in the inn."

"No room for them in the inn."

Martin Luther states that Mary and Joseph "were the most insignificant and despised, so that they had to make way for others until they were obliged to take refuge in a stable, to share with the cattle lodging, table, bedchamber, and bed, while many a wicked man sat at the head in the hotels and was honored as lord. No one noticed or was conscious of what God was doing in that stable . . . O what a dark night this was for Bethlehem, that was not conscious of that glorious light!"[12]

"Although Mary's critical situation was clear to all, no one gave up accommodation to her and Joseph . . . . The early church father Justin Martyr (A.D.150) states that this 'stable' was a cave. About A.D. 330, Constantine . . . caused a church to be built over this cave."[13] (This church still has services; it is the oldest practicing church.)

The area of this cave was used for bazaars and markets, where animals were killed and meat sold. It was a place for wine and cider to be stored. In fact, this cave was a more public place than we imagine. People were walking to and fro. Mary would have been in view of the public at large.

"He was born outside everything. Passed the court, passed the palace, passed the inn, passed the dwelling place . . . and was born into this world so low . . . that no baby could ever be born lower."[14]

---

11. Morgan, *Gospel According to Luke*, 35.
12. Miller, *Book of Jesus*, 121.
13. Geldenhuys, *International Commentary*, 101.
14. Morgan, *Gospel According to Luke*, 36.

*"She brought forth her firstborn Son, and
wrapped Him in swaddling clothes."*

"It is very beautiful, but oh, the pity of it, the tragedy of it, the loneliness of it; that in that hour of all hours, when a (woman) should be surrounded by the most tender care, she was alone. The method of the writer is very distinct. She with her own hands wrapped the baby round with those swaddling clothes and laid Him in the manger. There was no one to do it for her."[15] "The swaddling clothes, it is said, are used for grave clothes. Possibly, her veil or some article of (Mary's) clothing she could spare."[16]

This Anointed One, foretold, was born that night . . .

Notice the words "firstborn Son." "The simple meaning is that Jesus was her eldest child, the firstborn Son. But there is a larger meaning. Firstborn does not mean only first in time, it means also first in place, first in order, first in importance. In the New Testament He is called, 'Firstborn of creation.' He is called 'Firstborn from the dead.' He is called 'Firstborn of many brethren' . . . (and yet there is a more profound note). Who is this child? The Son of God. That is what happened in that manger. There in that little town of Bethlehem Ephratah, the Son of God, in human form, had entered the stream of human history."[17]

Verse 8: Shepherds

"And there were in the same country shepherds abiding in the field, keeping watch over their flock by night" (Luke 2:8).

"Somewhere in the fields near Bethlehem, where David many centuries before had also kept sheep, a small group of shepherds were keeping watch over their sheep."[18]

These were not ordinary shepherds. These shepherds watch the flocks destined for sacrificial services near the place consecrated and foretold by the prophet that the Messiah would be revealed.

15. Morgan, *Gospel According to Luke*, 36.

16. Miller, *Book of Jesus*, 121.

17. Morgan, *Gospel According to Luke*, 36.

18. Geldenhuys, *International Commentary*, 111.

Verse 9: Angel, Glory of the Lord

"And, lo, the angel of the Lord came upon them, and the glory of the Lord shone round about them: and they were sore afraid" (Luke 2:9).

Rabbinical tradition states that "wherever Michael appears, there also is the glory of the shekinah. . . . The glory of the Lord seemed to enwrap them, as in a mantle of light."[19] "The radiating glory of God's majesty became visible to them as it had appeared to Moses at the burning bush, to the Israelites in the pillar of fire in the desert . . . to the worshippers in the tabernacle or temple, or as it would later in becoming visible to the three disciples on the Mountain of Transfiguration."[20]

Verses 10–12: The Message

"And the angel said unto them, Fear not: for, behold, I bring you good tidings of great joy, which shall be to all people. For unto you is born this day in the city of David a Saviour, which is Christ the Lord. And this shall be a sign unto you; Ye shall find the babe wrapped in swaddling clothes, lying in a manger" (Luke 2:10–12).

Before the shepherds could respond or say a word . . .

Verses 13–14

"And suddenly there was with the angel a multitude of the heavenly host praising God, and saying, Glory to God in the highest and on earth peace, good will toward men" (Luke 2:13–14).

Only once before had the words of the angels' hymn fallen upon man's ears, when Isaiah "saw the Lord sitting on a throne, high and lifted up, and the train of His robe filled the temple . . . (and he heard the angelic host crying) Holy, holy, holy is the Lord of Hosts; the whole earth is full of His glory."

19. Edersheim, *Life and Times*, 187.
20. Geldenhuys, *International Commentary*, 111.

Verse 15a: Angels had gone away.

"And it came to pass, as the angels were gone away from them into heaven ..." (Luke 2:15a).

"The host of angels had appeared unexpectedly and suddenly, but (as indicated by the Greek) they departed gradually so that the shepherds could see them ascending to heaven. By this means they could better realize the actuality of what had happened ... As a result, there is no question of doubt with them concerning the truth of the tidings brought by the (angel). They know that the event has actually taken place and realize that it is the Lord who has sent them the (good news) through the angel."[21]

Verse 15–20

" ... the shepherds said one to another, Let us now go even unto Bethlehem, and see this thing which is come to pass, which the Lord hath made known unto us. And they came with haste, and found Mary, and Joseph, and the babe lying in a manger. And when they had seen it, they made known abroad the saying which was told them concerning this child. And all they that heard it wondered at those things which were told them by the shepherds. But Mary kept all these things, and pondered them in her heart. And the shepherds returned, glorifying and praising God for all the things that they had heard and seen, as it was told unto them" (Luke 2:15–20).

"The Magi (wise men), who would come much later, had a star to guide them. But all the shepherds had was the sign given them by the angels."[22] It took much time and effort to find the Christ Child.

Shepherding was the lowest of vocations at this time. They were on the lowest rung of society. Luther made this comment about the shepherds: "How very richly God honors those who are despised of men ... Here you see that His eyes look into the depths of humility, as is written, 'He sitteth above the cherubim' and looketh into the depths. Nor could the angels find princes or valiant men to whom to communicate the good news; but only unlearned laymen, the most humble people on earth. Could they not have addressed the high priest, who was supposed (to know) so much concerning God and the angels? No, God chose poor shepherds, who, though they were of low esteem in the sight of men, were in heaven

21. Geldenhuys, *International Commentary*, 187.
22. Wiersbe, *Expository Outlines*, 151.

regarded as worthy of such great grace and honor."[23] These humble shepherds saw with their own eyes the Promised One of Old.

They made "widely known" these events throughout Jerusalem and vicinity. Anna and Simeon probably heard through the shepherds the glorious news of the Christ child. Masses of people began to wonder about this strange and wonderful story. Could it be? Has He come? Has Isaiah's prophecy come true?

"For unto us a child is born, Unto us a Son is given" (Isa. 9:6). "To Us, to Us, to Us is born and to Us is given this Child."[24]

"For God so loved the world that He gave His only begotten Son, that whosoever believeth in him should not perish, but have everlasting life" (John 3:16).

This One, this Anointed One of Old, foretold by the prophets, came 2,000 years ago, born of a virgin. In the "fullness of time" the "Morning Star" appeared, the Eternal Son of God, God tabernacled in the flesh. As Mary kissed the brow of her baby boy, she was, in fact, kissing the very face of God.

How will you respond to this message? Will you, like the "inhabitants of Bethlehem did in . . . ignorance . . . (and like) many today in willful indifference . . . refuse to make room for the Son of God . . . to give no place to Him in their feelings, their affections, their thoughts, their views of life, their wishes, their decisions, their actions, or their daily conduct. And thus deny themselves the greatest privilege of all and incur the greatest loss to their lives."[25]

Paul wrote, "Thanks be to God for His indescribable gift!" (2 Cor. 9:15) This gift is His Son, the Messiah, the Anointed One, the Savior. "He that believeth on the Son hath everlasting life: and he that believeth not the Son shall not see life; but the wrath of God abideth on him" (John 3:36). Jesus said, " . . . I am the light of the world: he that followeth me shall not walk in darkness, but shall have the light of life" (John 8:12).

The greatest gift you can receive is the gift of eternal life through Jesus Christ our Lord. If you have never received Him as Saviour, please come with haste, like the shepherds; come quickly to see the Son of God. He is a free gift to you from the heavenly Father.

23. Miller, *Book of Jesus*, 122-123.

24. Miller, *Book of Jesus*, 123.

25. Geldenhuys, *International Commentary*, 102.

Christian, let our main focus be upon God's gift to us and may we like Mary treasure all these things and ponder them in our hearts.

"For God so loved the world that He gave H is only begotten Son . . . " And Jesus gave His all for us, though He being God . . . "made Himself of no reputation, taking the form of a bondservant, and coming in the likeness of men (so that we would understand) . . . humbled Himself and became obedient to . . . death, even the death of the cross" (Phil. 2:7–8 (NKJV)). And He rose on the third day.

"How else can we respond (to this?) But by giving ourselves to Him completely in return."[26] Come . . . and receive the gift.

26. MacArthur, *God with Us*, 134.

—— Chapter 6 ——

The Birth of God

Preface

THE ANCIENTS SAID WHEN the apostle John, the "Son of Thunder" who became a "disciple of love," was in his eighth and ninth decade of life, the Christians would literally carry him, because of his poor health, from church to church. The early Christian community wanted to hear what the last living apostle had to say. The pastors would ask the sage apostle, "Would you give us a word from the Lord?"

It is reported that John would simply say, "Love God with all your heart, love each other, and by this all men will know that you are Christ's disciples." John's focus was the love of God. In chapter one of his magnificent gospel account, we find the ultimate expression of God's love: God himself becoming man, dying on a cruel Roman cross, paying the price for redemption.

The great apostle takes us beyond the mountains, past the heavens, and exiting the sidereal universe, enters the heavenly chamber of the throne of God. There he kneels before God, looking into the heart of the eternal mind of the Almighty, and receives the revelation, thus recording, "In the beginning was the Word, and the Word was with God, and the Word was God."

In the next few pages, you will enter the mind of God and experience a universal paradigm shift in God's dealings with man, the incarnation (the birth of God in the flesh), and the birth of a movement that changed the world forever.

Part One: The Son of Thunder (John 1)

"The Fourth Gospel opens with a magnificent series of apparently meta-physical propositions. The time is the beginning of all things, the theme is the creation, and the substantives denote a sequence of large concepts: God, the Word, light, life, darkness."[1]

"The Gospel of John may be compared to an artesian well that never runs dry. From its depths there bubbles forth clear, refreshing water to quench the thirst of men and women who turn to it in their quest for life's true meaning."[2]

"Within John's Gospel we will find a universal impetus that declares that Jesus is the 'Savior of the world.' 'For we have heard Him ourselves, and know that this is indeed the Christ, the Saviour of the world' (John 4:42). John speaks of 'freedom, truth, and love.'"[3]

"Therefore if the Son makes you free, you shall be free indeed" (John 8:36).

John gives us the purpose for writing his Gospel: "And many other signs truly did Jesus in the presence of his disciples, which are not written in this book: But these are written, that ye might believe that Jesus is the Christ, the Son of God; and that believing ye might have life through his name" (20:30–31).

"This statement contains three basic affirmations:

1. The author's central message is related to Jesus, whom he presents to his readers as 'the Christ, the Son of God.'

2. There is an appeal for 'believing' in Jesus. This concept carries for John the connotation of trust and commitment as well as of intellectual assent to a statement of fact.

3. The result of such a personal and positive response will be 'life' in His name."[4]

The word *life* (Greek: *Zoe*) is the most significant word in the Gospel of John. It appears thirty-five times more than in any other Gospel. John's Gospel is also called the "Gospel of Life."

---

1. Harvey, *Jesus on Trial*, 18.
2. Vanderlip, *Christianity*, 9.
3. Vanderlip, *Christianity*, 12.
4. Vanderlip, *Christianity*, 17.

John's style is not so much a narrative of the Life of Christ as much as a series of sermonic themes and theological treatises which centers around the incarnation, seven miracles, seven "I Am's," faith, unbelief, light, darkness, truth, and life. John's passion is nothing less than profound.

Who Was John?

"In the book the author is identified as the 'beloved disciple' (21:20-24) who sat next to Jesus at the (last) supper. John . . . was the brother of James, another of the twelve disciples of Jesus, and both were sons of Zebedee. Like his father and older brother, James, he was a fisherman on the Sea of Galilee, and together with Peter and James, John was one of the three disciples closest to Jesus."[5]

Some historians state that John's family business made them relatively wealthy and influential which may explain how he was able to enter the house of Caiaphas during one of the trials of Jesus.

Jesus called James and John "sons of thunder" (Mark 3:17). They rebuked a man for casting out demons because he was not following them (Mark 9:38). Also, they asked permission to punish the Samaritans with fire from heaven for their inhospitality to Jesus. Later they urged Jesus to give the two of them places of honor in the kingdom to come.

Peter, James, and John witnessed events that not shared by the other apostles, such as the raising of Jairus's daughter, the transfiguration (John 1:14), and Jesus's prayer in the Garden of Gethsemane. According to Luke, it was Peter and John who were sent to prepare the Passover meal (Last Supper).

At the crucifixion, John appears standing with Mary, the mother of Jesus. From the cross, Jesus said to his mother, "Woman, behold your son!" (referencing John) and to the disciple, "Behold your mother!" And from that hour, that disciple took her to his own home. (19:26–27) Mary would have been in her late forties or early fifties at this point. She would live the rest of her natural life under the care of John, the beloved.

After Mary Magdalene reported that Jesus's tomb was empty, John with Peter ran to the tomb and, after seeing, believed. John was the first to accept Jesus's resurrection.

5. Bell, *Roots of Jesus*, 77.

Later, John was in the group that went fishing with Peter in Galilee. When Jesus appeared on the shore, the beloved disciple was the first to recognize him.

> "After these things Jesus shewed himself again to the disciples at the sea of Tiberias; and on this wise shewed he himself. There were together Simon Peter and Thomas called Didymus, and Nathanael of Cana in Galilee, and the sons of Zebedee, and two other of his disciples. Simon Peter saith unto them, I go a-fishing. They say unto him, we also go with thee. They went forth, and entered into a ship immediately; and that night they caught nothing. But when the morning was now come, Jesus stood on the shore: but the disciples knew not that it was Jesus. Then Jesus saith unto them, Children, have ye any meat? They answered him, No. And he said unto them, Cast the net on the right side of the ship, and ye shall find. They cast therefore, and now they were not able to draw it for the multitude of fishes. Therefore that disciple whom Jesus loved saith unto Peter, It is the Lord. Now when Simon Peter heard that it was the Lord he girt his fisher's coat unto him, (for he was naked,) and did cast himself into the sea. And the other disciples came in a little ship; (for they were not far from land, but as it were two hundred cubits,) dragging the net with fishes. As soon then as they were come to land, they saw a fire of coals there, and fish laid thereon, and bread. Jesus saith unto them, Bring of the fish which ye have now caught. Simon Peter went up, and drew the net to land full of great fishes, an hundred and fifty and three: and for all there were so many, yet was not the net broken. Jesus saith unto them, Come and dine. And none of the disciples durst ask him, Who art thou? knowing that it was the Lord. Jesus then cometh, and taketh bread, and giveth them, and fish likewise. This is now the third time that Jesus shewed himself to his disciples, after that he was risen from the dead" (John 21:1–14).

Perhaps John recalled Luke 5:1–11 when Jesus called them to "full-time" discipleship (apparently, they initially did not follow Him on a "full-time" basis (see *Bible Knowledge Commentary*)).

John's brother, James, was the first apostle to be martyred. John continued for some time as a prominent leader in the early Christian church. Paul lists John as one of the "pillars" (Gal. 2:9) of the Jerusalem church. His prominence is also recorded in the book of Acts, where he is said to have accompanied Peter on important missions. "Now when the apostles which were at Jerusalem heard that Samaria had received the word of God, they sent unto them Peter and John" (Acts 8:14).

John authored First, Second, and Third John, and later in his life he was exiled to the island of Patmos, after a failed attempt by the authorities to kill him by boiling him in oil in Ephesus. Terribly scarred, on this remote island John receives the Revelation of Jesus Christ, thus the title of the last book of the Bible.

Not only was John impetuous, desiring to destroy the Samaritans and coveting an honored position in the Kingdom, but he became a man of compassion and concern as he leaned upon the breast of our Lord at the Last Supper and asked, "Is it I who will betray You?" (Matt. 26:22)

He also became a man of commitment as he lovingly cared for Mary. He became a man of passion and zeal for the Lord as he cried with enthusiasm on that morning after the resurrection beholding the Master on the shore, "It is the Lord!"

This one, named John, became a "pillar" of the church. With the tenacity and strength of a fisherman and with the love of a seasoned apostle, he gave us an example of persevering until the end of our days, embracing truth with a passion manifesting a submission before a holy God. He demonstrated the manifest destiny of every believer when we shall appear before the presence of God (Rev. 1:9–18). John enters the presence of God with grace, dignity, and true spirituality in his Gospel.

Augustine writes that John was "among the mountains" when he wrote, "In the beginning was the Word, and the Word was with God, and the Word was God." What was this mountain like? How high was it? It surpassed all earthly summits, it surpassed all the spaces of the air, it surpassed the highest stars, and it surpassed all the choirs and all the legions of angels. If indeed it had not surpassed everything created, it would not have come to the One through whom everything has been made (John 1:3). You cannot realize what he surpassed unless you see where he arrived."[6] We will embrace with passion, meditation, and worship the first chapter of John's crowned "Gospel of Life."

We Can Change!

If our Lord can take a rough, crass, cursing fisherman and turn him into a vessel of honor and grace, He can surely change you and me.

6. Clark, *Augustine*, 269

THE BIRTH OF GOD

He will give hope to you who have no hope. "[L]ay hold upon the hope set before us. Which hope we have as an anchor of the soul, both sure and stedfast . . . even Jesus" (Heb. 6:18–20)

He will give peace to you who have no peace. Jesus said, "Peace I leave with you, My peace I give to you; not as the world gives do I give to you. Let not your heart be troubles, neither let it be afraid" (John 14:27).

He will give rest to the restless and lift your burden. Jesus also said, "Come to Me, all you who labor and are heavy laden, and I will give you rest. Take My yoke upon you and learn from Me, for I am gentle and lowly in heart, and you will find rest for your soul. For My yoke is easy and My burden is light" (Matt. 11:28–30).

He will give life to those who believe. "All things were made by Him; and without Him was not any thing made that was made" (John 1:3).

"The Father loveth the Son, and hath given all things into His hand. He that believeth on the Son hath everlasting life: and he that believeth not the Son shall not see life; but the wrath of God abideth on him" (John 3:35–36).

Choose this day what you will do. Will you believe?

Part Two: The Incarnation (John 1:1–18]

"In his classic 'A Tale of Two Cities,' Charles Dickens summarizes the era of the French Revolution:

'It was the best of times, it was the worst of times, it was the age of wisdom, it was the age of foolishness, it was the epoch of belief, it was the epoch of incredulity, it was the season of light, it was the season of darkness, it was the spring of hope, it was the winter of despair, we had everything before us, we had nothing before us, we were all going direct to Heaven, we were all going direct the other way.'

With this prologue Dickens prefaces his drama. Before the curtain rises, he introduces us to some of the novel's major themes: prosperity and poverty, light and darkness, hope and despair.

John also introduces his Gospel with a prologue. R.C.H. Lenski, in his commentary on the Gospel of John, sees this eighteen-verse introduction as some of the most scintillating writing in the entire New Testament: 'John's is the paragon among the Gospels, 'the one, tender, real crown-gospel of them all' (Luther), and the prologue is the central jewel set in pure gold.'

Like Dickens's introduction, John's prologue gives us a glimmer of the book's major themes: the deity of Christ, Christ as light and life, the world shrouded in darkness, the witness of John the Baptist, rejection and acceptance of the Savior, and examples of the glory, grace, and truth of Christ."[7]

Cousin John

John the Baptist would have known Jesus personally as a little boy since John was the Lord's cousin. His mother, Elizabeth, was related to the Virgin Mary. The strange, and mysterious, and other worldly circumstances surrounding the birth of Jesus in Bethlehem were no secret to the family. Undoubtedly, during his childhood and early years of manhood, Jesus, along with his brothers, sisters, and cousins, would have had normal family contact. Celebrating the feasts and annual pilgrimages to Jerusalem and celebrating birthdays along with other special occasions would have been an opportunity to spend time together, laughing, catching up on the latest family news, and seeing old friends. When John, the son of Zebedee, became a disciple of Jesus, he knew that the virgin-born Jesus of Nazareth was God. In his gospel, he simply tells us what he knows.

In John's prologue, his statement of thesis contains two parts—first, the essential declarations which are found in verses one, fourteen, and eighteen; and second, certain statements which are parenthetical.

Verse 1: "In the beginning was the Word, and the Word was with God, and the Word was God"

Verse 14: "And the Word was made flesh, and dwelt among us, and we beheld His glory, the glory as of the only begotten of the Father, full of grace and truth."

Verse 18: "No man hath seen God at any time; the only begotten Son, which is in the bosom of the Father, He hath declared Him."

Verse One

"In the beginning was the Word" "[r]ecalls the opening words of Genesis 1:1—'In the beginning God created the heavens and the earth.' The

---

7. Swindoll, *Exalting Christ*, 9.

expression does not refer to a particular moment of time but assumes a timeless eternity."[8]

Word is the Greek "logos." Greek philosophers were familiar with this word. Philo, a Jewish philosopher, borrowed and used this word for his own purposes. The Greek mind used the word as a reference for the abstract components that are foundational to everything that would be considered solid, concrete, a sure foundation. The word "logos" for the Greek would point to what we would call wisdom.

John did not borrow the Greek concept of "logos," nor did he borrow any of Philo's ideas to describe Jesus. He used a more Hebraic concept. The Hebrews had a more sophisticated approach to the eternal verities behind space and time. The Hebrews would argue from the thought to the thinker, from wisdom to God. The Greeks did not go that far. Thus, when John calls Jesus "the Word," the Logos, he is referring to him as the thinker, the omniscient genius behind the created universe.[9]

Was in the Greek is in the imperfect tense, which suggests not something past, present, or future, but something continuous. The idea is an existence that transcends time, that which is beyond time or space. People measure existence by time. Our point of reference is a point in time, an earmark, a high water mark. The verb John uses takes us beyond this dimension of time and into a timeless sphere of reality. In other words, the One John calls "the Word," the Logos, doesn't belong to time and space, but rather, the Word belongs to timelessness, a reality where there is no measure other than God. The Logos did not have a beginning nor will it have an ending. The "Word" is eternal. The "Word" is everlasting, without time, space, or measure.

"We can go back in our minds quite easily a century or two, even a millennium or two. Astronomers have accustomed themselves to think in terms of billions of years. But to go back beyond the beginning, to no beginning at all—that is disquieting. But, says John, when we think of Jesus, that is where we must begin. We must go back to the dateless past, to a time before time. We must think of Jesus as never having begun at all. He is eternally God."[10]

With is the Greek "Pros"—face to face; interfacing; having intercourse; communing; the closest relationship; at home; intimate association with

8. Tenney, *Expositor's Bible*.

9. Phillips, *Exploring John*, 16.

10. Phillips, *Exploring John*, 17.

God; partaking of the essence of God; God in triune being; with God; is God. The Greek text stresses description rather than individualization. Meaning this: "the Word was deity, one with God, rather than 'a god' or another being of the same class. This is the real meaning of the phrase. Unity of nature rather than similarity or likeness is implied. The external co-existence and unity of the Word with God is unmistakably asserted."[11]

Verse Fourteen

"And the Word became flesh"—With a few words, John draws the curtain open and reveals the heart of this new Christian faith, that which is unprecedented in human history, God becoming man to redeem us from our sin, and God taking on flesh so that we might understand, believe, and receive eternal life.

A NEW FORM

Became "refers, not to the beginning of something new, but to that which already had existence, as it became new in manifestation."[12] The "Logos" took on a new form, not a new existence. The birth of the Lord Jesus was unique. When a child is born, it is the creation of a new person, a new personality, someone who has never existed before, a new life. Not so with Jesus. The Word, Logos, or Jesus came into this world, already existing before the world was created, before Mary was born, before the Roman Empire. Jesus was not the creation of a new life, rather the continuance of a person who had existed in eternity past. Jesus did not cease to be God. He simply became human, completely human and completely God. This was something profoundly new in the history of the universe that caused heaven to pause in awe and the angelic host to sing, blinding earth's sidereal view, rumbling through Judea's hillside with the chorus, "Glory to God in the highest."

There was unity of the Godhead before and after the incarnation. Jesus did not cease to be God. At the same time, his humanity was real and complete. Jesus remained God as before, but "He became flesh."

11. Tenney, *Expositor's Bible*, 28.
12. Morgan, *Gospel According to John*, 23.

JESUS—TABERNACLE

Dwelt among us literally means "to pitch a tent, to dwell temporarily." Or, He tabernacled among us. Some believe that because of the word *tabernacle* that the incarnation took place on the joyous annual Jewish Feast of Tabernacles. I believe John's use of the word *tabernacle* points to a rich typology of the Old Testament tabernacle.

Arthur W. Pink states in his work, *Exposition of the Gospel of John,*

1. "The tabernacle was a temporary appointment and was used in the wilderness. The wilderness strikingly foreshadowed the conditions amid which the eternal Word tabernacled among men at His first advent. The wilderness home of the tabernacle unmistakably foreshadowed the manger-cradle, the Nazarene's Bench, the 'nowhere' for the Son of Man to lay His head, the borrowed tomb for His sepulchre. A careful study of the chronology of the Pentateuch seems to indicate that Israel used the tabernacle in the wilderness . . . less than thirty-five years.

2. The tabernacle was God's dwelling place and therefore the place where God met with men. 'There is one Mediator between God and men—the Man Christ Jesus' (1 Tim. 2:5).

3. The tabernacle was the center of Israel's camp. 'Where two or three are gathered together in My name, there am I in the midst of them' (Matt. 18:20).

4. The tabernacle was the place where the Law was preserved. Jesus came to fulfill the Law, not destroy it.

5. The tabernacle was the place where sacrifice was made. The body in which Jesus was tabernacled on earth was nailed to a cross where His precious blood was shed, and where complete atonement was made for sin.

6. The tabernacle was the place where the priestly family was fed and was the place of worship. Jesus is the Bread of Life. He is the One upon whom our soul delights to feed. The Church is God's priestly family today (1 Pet. 2:5). Christ is our food, our sustenance.

In terms of worship, it is 'by Him' we are to offer unto God a sacrifice of praise (Heb. 13:15). It is in Him, and by Him, alone, that we can worship the Father. It is through Him we have access to the throne of grace."[13]

13. Pink, *Exposition*, 34 and 37.

The tabernacle's glory and beauty was found within. From without, to the eye of the passersby, the structure looked like an ordinary tent set apart from the other tents, larger in size, yes, but rather ordinary. The furniture of the outer court was made of brass or simply copper. The curtains of the outer court were white, bleached by the sun. The only suggestion of beauty was found looking through the gate at the brazen altar. Even when the tabernacle was moved from place to place, the golden furniture found within was covered so that no one could behold the splendor of the sacred items.

This reminds us of the hidden glory of Christ Jesus. When he came to "pitch His tent" in the middle of humanity, He did not lay His deity aside, rather He covered His glory among us. The prophet said regarding the Messiah, "He has no form or comeliness; and when we see Him, there is no beauty that we should desire Him" (Isa. 53:2). The Apostle Paul stated, "Let this mind be in you, which was also in Christ Jesus; Who, being in the form of God, thought it not robbery to be equal with God; But made Himself of no reputation, and took upon Him the form of a servant, and was made in the likeness of men: And being found in fashion as a man, He humbled Himself, and became obedient unto death, even the death of the cross" (Phil. 2:5–8).

"The inside of the tabernacle, seen only by the priests, was glorious. The inner hangings were of blue, purple, and scarlet, and were fine linen. All the inner furniture was of gold or overlaid with gold. That mysterious shekinah cloud, which overshadowed the camp of Israel, came to rest on the mercy seat in the Holy of Holies, where it bathed all with the light and glory of another world."[14]

GRACE & TRUTH

"We beheld His glory, the glory as of the only begotten (the one and only) of the Father." They saw His glory manifested on the Mount of Transfiguration. This is the same glory that appeared on Mt. Sinai "full of grace and truth."

Moses asked of God, "[S]how me thy glory . . . " The reply was "I will make all my goodness pass before you, and will proclaim before you My name . . . " (Exod. 33:18–19).

"And the Lord descended in the cloud, and stood with him there, and proclaimed the name of the Lord. And the Lord passed by before him, and

14. Phillips, *Exploring John*, 27.

proclaimed, the Lord, The Lord God, merciful and gracious, longsuffering, and abundant in goodness and truth" (Exod. 34:5–6).

Mercy or goodness and truth (Hebrew: Chesed and Emeth) points us to the goodness and the glory of God. The Greek words that John uses in John 1:14, "full of grace (charis), and truth (aletheia)," are understood to be a rendering of the last words of Exodus 34:6. Therefore, the glory seen in Christ, the incarnate Word, was the same glory that was revealed to Moses on Mount Sinai; however, now, that glory became human, fully God & fully man, "full of grace and truth."

"Grace has two basic meanings to it. One, of unmerited and undeserved favor, something we could never achieve, earn or attain. The fact that God came to earth to live and to die for our sins, for atonement. The other reflects the modern Greek meaning of 'charis,' meaning charm. Simply, 'in Jesus men are confronted with the sheer loveliness of the love of God.'"[15]

The Hebrew word for truth is *emet* which is comprised of the first, middle, and last letters of the Hebrew alphabet—aleph, mem, and tav— meaning totality. In other words, "truth" embraces the beginning, middle and end of all there is. "Truth" in the gospel of John speaks of the totality of God or God's reality. Jesus said, "I am the truth," meaning that truth is not simply teachings that come from Jesus, though they are truth, but rather Jesus Himself is the totality of truth. God, who is the Creator, is the only true reality. The reality of God is revealed in the person of Jesus. Therefore, truth is Christ Jesus, as we are "complete in Him."

The nature of truth is exclusive. The opposite of truth is false. If Jesus is not truth, then He is false. When Pilate asked Jesus, "Art thou the King of the Jews?"

Jesus answered him by saying, "Sayest thou this thing of thyself, or did others tell it thee of me?" (John 18:33–34) Basically, Jesus was saying to Pilate, "Look deep within your heart Pilate, the answer may be difficult for you to receive. Are you ready to deal with implications of my answer?"

"Pilate therefore said unto him, art thou a king then? Jesus answered, Thou sayest that I am a king. To this end was I born, and for this cause came I into the world, that I should bear witness unto the truth. Every one that is of the truth heareth my voice" (John 18:37).

To reject Jesus is to embrace falsehood, or to believe a lie. Jesus said, "If ye continue in my word, then are ye my disciples indeed; and ye shall know the truth, and the truth shall make you free" (John 8:31–32). The

15. Barclay, *Gospel of John*, 47.

enemy of our soul is the "father of all lies" (John 8:44). He will do anything to keep us from coming to the truth, to God Himself.

Pilate asks, "What is truth?" Notice "no answer is given in words, but the Passion narrative gives the answer in deeds . . . It is finished! Truth as Jesus understood it was a costly affair."[16]

Verse Eighteen

"No man hath seen God at any time; the only begotten Son, which is in the bosom of the Father, He hath declared Him."

This verse declares what Jesus revealed. The expression "the bosom of the Father" is a most beautiful and intimate expression, between a child and a parent, or a friend and a friend. The revelation that Jesus came to unveil was nothing less than the heart of God. Jesus could have come as a sage, warrior, or king, thus revealing the Father in a different way. Instead, Jesus revealed the bosom of the Father, the heart of God. "For God so loved the world that He gave . . . " (John 3:16).

"He has declared Him" is from the Greek word, where we derive the term exegesis, which means to explain or interpret. Jesus has made known things that men had not seen.

"The life and words of Jesus are more than an announcement; they are an explanation of God's attitude toward men and of His purpose for them."[17]

Simply, John was saying as we arrange his words . . . "In the beginning was the Word and the Word was with God, and the Word was God."

No one has seen God at any time. "And the Word became flesh and dwelt (pitched His tent) among us . . . full of grace and truth."

The only begotten Son, who is in the bosom of the Father, He has declared Him.

Jesus is Lord . . . Jesus is Truth.

Part Three: The Prophet (John 1)

Author John Phillips writes, "From out of the wilderness had come striding a spiritual giant of a man. His dress, diet, deportment and demands made

16. Morris, *Gospel According to John*, 260–61.

17. Tenney, *Expositor's Bible*, 34.

his hearers think of Elijah. His voice thundered until the windows of conscience rattled in everyone's soul. His eyes flashed like lightning, seeming to read the secrets of everyone's heart.

Multitudes heard about this new prophet and flocked to hear him. The religious establishment investigated him, disliked him, feared him, rejected him, and was denounced by him. Herod on his throne was afraid of him. John the Baptist was his name—the son of a priest, (who was) married to the daughter of a priest.

His birth had been foretold. He had been raised strictly, with a view to his becoming a priest. He had also been raised as a Nazarite, with a view to his becoming a prophet. There already were priests after the order of Aaron—enough and to spare. Few and far between were prophets after the order of Elijah. What Israel needed was not another priest. What Israel needed was a prophet. John, by birth, training, disposition, conviction, and choice was raised up by God to be that prophet, the last of a long, illustrious line."[18]

John's message electrified the nation: "the Christ is coming! Repent! The kingdom of heaven is at hand!" Thousands throughout the land came to listen to him and were baptized.

John's parents, Zacharias and Elizabeth, were older people, not expecting to have a baby. "And they had no child, because that Elisabeth was barren, and they both were now well stricken in years" (Luke 1:7).

Luke tells us that John lived in the deserts most of his life. "And the child grew, and waxed strong in spirit, and was in the deserts till the day of his shewing unto Israel' (Luke 1:80).

John's clothing was made of camel's hair, he wore a leather belt, and his diet consisted of locusts and wild honey. "And John was clothed with camel's hair, and with a girdle of a skin about his loins; and he did eat locusts and wild honey" (Mark 1:6).

John was the last Old Testament prophet —just a man. There was nothing unique about his name. He was just John . . . but he was not ordinary. He fulfilled an important purpose.

Sent From God

Verse 6: "There was a man sent from God, whose name was John."

18. Phillips, *Exploring John*, 35.

"*There was a man*": The Greek emphasizes, "There appeared on the stage of history, in a specific fixed position in place, time or space."

"*Sent from God, whose name was John.*" John the Baptist was both a priest and Nazarite. There are only three Nazarites mentioned in the Bible: Samuel, Samson, and John the Baptist. A Nazarite could not touch a dead body or the fruit of the vine and had to let his hair grow long. He thus proclaimed to the world that his affections, appetite, and appearance were on the altar dedicated to the Lord. By doing so, he kept his body in subjection. This lifestyle was difficult to live. The standard and devotion to God was higher than what the average follower of God could bear. Therefore, in the fifteen hundred years of Jewish history, we read only of three who were set apart for God in such a manner. Samson, who failed miserably, was one. The other two, Samuel and John the Baptist, were Hebrew prophets. Samuel was the first of the prophets, and John was the last.

Witnessing the Light

Verse 7: "The same came for a witness, to bear witness of the Light, that all men through him might believe."

"*Through him*": Or in other words, through John. It is interesting to note that technically it was John who first pointed men to Jesus as the light and hope of the World. Subsequently, it was through the belief of these people that others came to believe in Jesus as the Messiah. Therefore, all believers have, in this sense, been first brought to faith by John.

Verse 8: "He was not that Light, but was sent to bear witness of that Light."

John the Apostle may have been making a strong point to combat those in his day who were making exaggerated claims about John the Baptist.

Verse 15: "John bare witness of Him and cried, saying, This was He of whom I spake, He that cometh after me is preferred before me: for He was before me."

John the Baptist was the first to identify the Lord Jesus for who He really was. He recognized the Lord's pre-existence—the One of old foretold.

The word *before* (Greek, protos) "has reference to time—not just to priority of birth, but rather to uniqueness in the matter of time. The Lord Jesus related Himself in time in quite a different way from any other human being. He was related to time as one coming out of eternity. As to His

THE BIRTH OF GOD

mother, He was born as a baby in Bethlehem; as to His Father, He was 'the Ancient of Days.'"[19]

Who are You?

Verse 19: "And this is the record of John, when the Jews sent priests and Levites from Jerusalem to ask him, Who art thou?"

"Here for the first time we come upon the use of the term 'the Jews' in (John). This term denotes not the people as a whole but one particular group—here, the religious establishment in Jerusalem, whether the Sanhedrin or the temple authorities.

Elsewhere, it is occasionally used ('After these things Jesus walked in Galilee: for He would not walk in Jewry, because the Jews sought to kill Him.' John 7:1) to mean the Judeans as distinct from the Galileans, while at other times it has quite a general meaning."[20]

This is the only time we find the two orders, "priests and Levites," named together in the New Testament. In verse twenty-four we learn that they came from Jerusalem and were sent by the Pharisees.

At this time there was great Messianic expectation and John's ministry was stirring the countryside. John did not fit into any religious mold that was familiar to the Jewish authorities. John's obvious popularity and success demanded an explanation.

Verse 20–21: "And he confessed, and denied not; but confessed, I am not the Christ. And they asked him, what then? Art thou Elias? And he saith, I am not. Art thou that prophet? And he answered, no."

John disclaimed the title of Messiah, meaning anointed. It was a title that associated political freedom from oppressors. Perhaps John did not want to be connected to any political purview. Simply, John did not want to be seen as an insurrectionist. Because of John's roughened exterior many believed him to be Elijah personified. Elijah had challenged Ahab (1 Kgs 17–19), and was prophesied to come preparing the way for the Messiah (Mal. 3).

Are you the Prophet? They were probably referring to God's word to Moses: "The Lord your God will raise up for you a prophet like me from among your own brothers. You must listen to him" (Deut. 18:15). This

---

19. Phillips, *Exploring John*, 29.
20. Bruce, *Gospel of John*, 46.

71

prophecy said he would be like Moses; therefore, the Jews were inquiring whether John would lead them in a New Exodus and overcome the Romans.

It is interesting how John's answers became shorter with each question.

Verse 22: "Then said they unto him, Who art thou? That we may give an answer to them that sent us. What sayest thou of thyself?"

After his denials, the delegation from Jerusalem, being greatly frustrated demanded, "Who are you? What do you say about yourself?"

The Voice

Verse 23: "He said, I am the voice of one crying in the wilderness, Make straight the way of the Lord, as said the prophet Esaias."

"Voice of one . . . make straight the way . . . " John was the subject of Old Testament prophecy (Isaiah 40). The fortieth chapter of Isaiah deals with prophecies regarding the future. There will be someone who prepares a road for the king through hilly and rugged territory, so that he can travel over a smooth road. John calls himself the "road-builder" for one greater than he, the Messiah. John's birth was miraculous as God intervened (Luke 1:7, 13); he was filled with the Holy Spirit from his mother's womb (Luke 1:15); he was sent from God (John 1:6); he prepared the way of the Lord (Matthew 3:3). The Lord said of John, "Among them that are born of women there has not risen a greater than John the Baptist . . . '" (Matt. 11:11).

Who are you, John? He had quite a résumé. However, his purpose was not to draw people to himself, but rather, he desired men to follow Jesus, the coming Anointed One.

John was a voice, but he was not the Word. As the Word exists in the mind before the voice articulates, so it was that the Word (Logos) was before the voice.

"Make straight the way of the Lord."

John told us specifically who this One would be. This One who is coming is the Lord. He used the word *Jehovah*. Jesus of Nazareth, the one born in Bethlehem, is none other than God Himself in flesh, who came to bring redemption, forgiveness, and hope.

Isaiah 40:1–8: "Comfort ye, comfort ye my people, saith your God. Speak ye comfortably to Jerusalem, and cry unto her, that her warfare is accomplished, that her iniquity is pardoned: for she hath received of the Lord's hand double for all her sins. The voice of him that crieth in the wilderness, Prepare ye the way of the Lord, make straight in the desert a highway for our God. Every valley shall be exalted, and every mountain and hill shall be made low: and the crooked shall be made straight, and the rough places plain: And the glory of the Lord shall be revealed, and all flesh shall see it together: for the mouth of the Lord hath spoken it. The voice said, Cry. And he said, what shall I cry? All flesh is grass, and all the goodliness thereof is as the flower of the field; The grass withereth, the flower fadeth: because the Spirit of the Lord bloweth upon it: surely the people is grass. The grass withereth, the flower fadeth: but the word of our God shall stand for ever."

All flesh is grass—You may say, "This isn't very comforting." You must understand this is how God begins to comfort us. Because of our pride and selfishness, God must remind us of our lowly estate, our sinfulness, our neediness. God must prick our conscience to get our attention. That is why Peter bridged Isaiah 40 with the gospel message of redemption: "For all flesh is as grass, and all the glory of man as the flower of grass. The grass withereth, and the flower thereof falleth away: but the word of the Lord endureth for ever. And this is the word which by the gospel is preached unto you" (1 Pet. 1: 24–25).

Why do we need the Lord and to be born again? Because "that which is born of the flesh is flesh" and "all flesh is as grass." Why do we need a new life? Because we are under judgment, because of sin, and this life is soon going to pass away, and we will stand before God in judgment, as "it is appointed unto man once to die, but after this the judgment." Only the word of the Lord endures forever; therefore, we must take heed and recognize how we need life from God—"He that hath the Son hath life."

We can understand how John sees himself in the prophetic passage of Isaiah 40. He says, this is who I am, simply, "a voice crying in the wilderness."

Verse 24–25: "And they which were sent were of the Pharisees. And they asked him, and said unto him, why baptizest thou then, if thou be not that Christ, nor Elias, neither that prophet?"

Isn't that the way it is? What do people do when they are taken out of their comfort zone with a new concept? They raise a ritualistic, familiar technicality.

One Among You

Verse 26: "John answered them, saying, I baptize with water: but there standeth one among you, whom ye know not;"

John's reply was succinct, "I baptize with water. That is all."

"The emphatic 'I baptize with water,' prepares (hearer) for the mention of someone else who will baptize in a different medium. For the moment, John does not speak of this different baptism, but he does speak of the One who will administer it."[21]

The religious leaders knew what John's baptism had meant. An outward sign of their repentance, confession of guilt, and their need for remission of sins. But John stated profoundly, "There stands One among you whom you do not know." Jesus was standing in the crowd that day, and yet John did not point him out. The reason could have been because Passover was about to begin and John had a special title to bestow upon the Lord. But he did definitely declared, "There stands One among you" (verse 26).

John said he was not the Christ, nor Elijah; I am not the prophet; however, "I am the voice of one crying in the wilderness. I am preparing the way of the Lord." He did not reveal the mission of the Christ that day. Yes, he affirmed that Christ came. However, he waited until the next day to declare who the Messiah was. "There stands One among you whom you do not know."

Israel was not ready to receive the message of God's redeeming grace through Jesus Christ our Lord. Also, today, in a post-Christian and post-modern era, many are unaware that there is One among (us) whom (they) do not know.

Verse 27: "He it is, who coming after me is preferred before me, whose shoe's latchet I am not worthy to unloose."

"John underlines his own relative unimportance in comparison with the Coming One, by saying that he is unfit even to perform such a lowly service as untying His sandal strap for Him. (in Jewish thought), 'Every service which a slave performs for his master, a disciple will perform for his teacher, except to untie his sandal strap.' Thus, John thought himself unworthy to perform even this act for the Coming One. But, in fact, in preparing the way for the Lord, John was discharging a far more honorable ministry than any of his hearers could have realized."[22]

Beyond Jordan

Verse 28: "These things were done in Bethabara beyond Jordan, where John was baptizing."

21. Bruce, *Gospel of John*, 50–51.
22. Bruce, *Gospel of John*, 51.

There is a reason why the Holy Spirit was pleased to tell us where this scene unfolded. Some scholars believe "Bethabara" is the place identical with "Bethbarah," mentioned in Judges 7:24, meaning "House of Passage" and so named to memorialize the crossing of the Jordan in the days of Joshua.

"And Gideon sent messengers throughout all Mount Ephraim, saying, Come down against the Midianites, and take before them the waters unto Bethbarah and Jordan. Then all the men of Ephraim gathered themselves together, and took the waters unto Bethbarah and Jordan" (Judg. 7:24).

It was here, the very same place where the Israelites crossed over the Jordan into the promised land, at a place whose name signified "House of Passage," a symbol of death and a symbol of life, that John was baptizing those who confessed and repented from their sins, dying to self, passing out of a false religion into the true faith, thus receiving eternal life. The meaning of this should not be hard to find. Those who believed became part of the remnant who were "prepared for the Lord" (Luke 1:17). So then, the place where John was baptizing was called "The House of Passage."

Behold

Verses 29–30: "The next day John seeth Jesus coming unto him, and saith, Behold the Lamb of God, which taketh away the sin of the world. This is He of whom I said, After me cometh a man which is preferred before me: for He was before me."

About six weeks beforehand, Jesus had been baptized by John in the Jordan River at this very spot. Subsequently, the Lord had gone into the Judean wilderness for forty days where He was tempted by Satan. John picks up the account after the temptation takes place. Jesus has returned to the Jordan, and on that day, the delegation arrived pressing John for answers. John had seen Jesus in the crowd; however, it wasn't until the next day that John revealed who Jesus was.

At this time of year, Passover was near. This feast commemorated the exodus, Israel's flight from Egypt, the birth of a nation, and redemption by the blood of the lamb. John did not introduce Jesus as the Messiah, Son of Man, nor the Son of God, nor the Word of God. He introduced Jesus as "Lamb of God who takes away the sin of the world." He targeted the heart of everyone's need—redemption. Jesus is the Lamb of God who can redeem you, if you believe.

John's baptism reminded people of their need to repent. However, people need more than just repentance, they need redemption. Water cannot remove the stain of sin, only blood can do that. Not the blood of bulls and goats (Heb. 10:1–4). Not religion. Only through the precious blood of the Lamb of God can one receive redemption.

John's title for the Lord, "Lamb," can be found twice in the Old Testament, twice in the Gospels, once in the book of Acts, once in the epistles and twenty-eight times in the book of Revelation. Isaac asked the question, as he and his father Abraham headed for the south side of Moriah, "Where is the lamb?" (Gen. 22:7). Abraham answered him, "God will provide Himself a lamb."

John answered Isaac's question, "Behold the Lamb of God." As these words came forth from John's mouth, you could hear the bleating of sheep in the background as they were being herded to Jerusalem. These sheep would be used for Passover sacrifice. John is saying in essence, "You hear the sheep in the background? See the sheep? I want you to see and hear the true Passover Lamb. He is the one who can redeem you. Behold, Jesus of Nazareth, the Lamb of God who takes away the sin of the world. It is He who can take away your sins. See Him. Hear Him. Follow Him."

Before Me

Verse 30: "This is He of whom I said, After me cometh a man which is preferred before me: for He was before me."

Notice the word *man* (Greek, *aner*, not *anthropos*). John repeats verse fifteen with exception of the word *man*, which emphasizes not only Christ's mannishness, His humanity, but His headship over His followers. This is the third time John declares that Christ was preferred before him (verses 15, 27, 30). He was affirming Christ's pre-existence.

Verse 31: "And I knew him not: but that He should be manifest to Israel, therefore am I come baptizing with water."

John knew Him, for they were cousins; however he did not know who He was until God revealed it to him.

Verse 32–33: "And John bare record, saying, I saw the Spirit descending from heaven like a dove, and it abode upon Him. And I knew Him not: but He that sent me to baptize with water, the same said unto me, Upon whom thou shalt see the Spirit descending, and remaining on Him, the same is He which baptizeth with the Holy Ghost."

This has reference to when the Lord himself was baptized by John in the Jordan, when the Father testified to His pleasure, in the Son, and when the Spirit descended upon Him as a dove. The dove manifested the character of the One on whom He came.

The dove is a symbol of love and sorrow. This is an appropriate emblem of the Messiah. Both His love and sorrow were manifested at Calvary. Thus, the heavenly Dove bears witness to the mission of Christ. Jesus was the perfect Lamb and a perfect sacrifice.

In contrast, when the Holy Spirit came upon the disciples on the Day of Pentecost, we read, "There appeared unto them cloven tongues like as of fire, and it sat upon each of them" (Acts 2:3).

Fire is a symbol of divine judgment. There was that in the disciples which needed to be judged. Sin was still present in the disciples, as their evil nature remained within them. However, there was nothing in the holy Lamb of God that needed judged. Therefore, the Holy Spirit descended upon Him like a dove, not as fire.

A New Paradigm

The gospels of Matthew, Mark, and Luke mention the Lord Jesus being anointed by the Holy Spirit at His baptism, but John is the only gospel writer that says the Spirit "abode" or "remained" upon Him. The Holy Spirit did not come upon Him and then leave again, such as in the Old Testament era. The word "abode" or "remain" speaks of continuing fellowship, not a temporary moment. The paradigm in the universe had shifted; a new era had begun.

John's baptism was an outward sign of inward repentance and confession, but there is a greater baptism. "For John truly baptized with water; but ye shall be baptized with the Holy Ghost not many days hence" (Acts 1:5). This is through trusting in the shed blood of the Lamb of God.

Notice again verse 29 of John 1—"The next day John seeth Jesus coming unto him, and saith, Behold the Lamb of God, which taketh away the sin of the world."

Isaiah stated that the Messiah, the Lamb of God, "was wounded for our transgressions, He was bruised for our iniquities: the chastisement of our peace was upon Him; and with His stripes we are healed."

Notice John said "sin," not sins. Sins are only the result of a cause— the Fall of Man and subsequent sin nature. The Lamb of God came not only to take away the individual's sins, but to take away or deal with the cause of sin as a whole.

The Apostle Paul said, "God hath made Him to be sin for us, who knew no sin." He not only bore our sins, and He not only atoned for all our acts of sin, but He died for what we are, sinners.

Whether we like it or not, within the heart of each of us is the propensity to sin. We are capable to flesh out the worse act of sin ever committed. We are sinners by nature. Sin dwells within us. Christ died to put away sin, not merely our sinful acts, through the sacrifice of Himself on the cross. The scripture states we are all sinners. God took that into account as Christ, who knew no sin, became sin on the cross. He took our place. He was made sin for us, and sin, the barrier between God and man, was taken away. What does this mean? Anyone, even the worst vilest sinner, can come into the presence of God and find forgiveness through Christ Jesus. Do you know the Lamb of God who takes away the sin of the world?"

A Declaration of Hope

Verse 34: "And I saw, and bare record that this is the Son of God."
John declared seven things:

1. Christ pre-existed in eternity past—verse 15.

2. Christ is Lord—verse 23.

3. Christ is above all—verse 27.

4. Christ is the Passover Lamb—verse 29.

5. Christ is without sin, morally perfect—verse 32.

6. Christ has a divine right to baptize with the Holy Spirit—verse 33.

7. Christ is the Son of God—verse 34.

Oh, how this world needs God's people to stand with a firm conviction as to what they believe, manifesting what it means to be a Christian. Will you take the Banner of Christ as John did and raise it high so that the world will see and believe?

Part Four: A New Movement Begins

"Again the next day after John stood, and two of his disciples; And looking upon Jesus as he walked, he saith, Behold the Lamb of God! And the two disciples heard him speak, and they followed Jesus. Then Jesus turned, and saw them following, and saith unto them, What seek ye? They said unto him, Rabbi, (which is to say, being interpreted, Master,) where dwellest thou? He saith unto them, Come and see. They came and saw where he dwelt, and abode with him that day: for it was about the tenth hour" (John 1:35–39).

Verse 35: "Next day"

This is the third day in a series of days. The first day is when the delegation came (1:19). The second day is when John declared Jesus to be the Lamb of God (1:29). This is the third day in which important decisions will be made.

Verse 36: "Looking at Jesus" (The Greek means "to fix one's gaze" or "to give a penetrating look.")

This word occurs only one other time in verse 42, where Jesus beheld Simon and said, "You will be called Cephas." This may have been the last time John the Baptist saw Jesus personally. John's fixed gaze on Jesus was followed by the exclamation, "Behold the Lamb of God." John's disciples will now be directed toward Jesus.

Verse 37: "Two disciples"

One was Andrew, and the other was John. In the gospel, John speaks as an eyewitness, though he does not directly give his name.

The First Question

Verse 38: "What do you seek?"

The Lord, knowing that He was being followed by disciples of John, turned and asked these two awkward fishermen, "What do you seek?" John and Andrew were in awe of the One they were following. John the Baptist, after all, declared Jesus to be the Passover Lamb of God. They had the chutzpah to follow Him, but they were probably afraid to speak to Jesus. So Jesus broke the silence with a penetrating question. In essence Jesus was asking, "Why are you seeking me? What do you want?"

"(This) is the very first word that is recorded as falling from the lips of Jesus as He began His public ministry. Here then was and is the first question, the first question of Jesus to a human being. The first question of Jesus to humanity as He begins His ministry. 'What do you seek?' It is a question that plumbs the deepest thing in human life. What are you seeking? What are you seeking? Here in the sanctuary, with the open Bible in front of us, or tomorrow in the store, the office, the home, that is the supreme question. What do we want? What are we seeking?"[23] What are we seeking in life?

Let's Do Lunch

"Where are you staying?" As though Andrew and John were saying "Aah! We don't know. Can we get back with you on that? Where do you live? Perhaps we can come by later and talk about it . . . Let's do lunch." All they knew is that John told them He is the One to follow. So they said, "Okay." They were probably in their twenties, not more than thirty years of age.

Verse 39: "Come and see"

"Come and see" or "Come, and you will see." The first two statements of Jesus in his public ministry were "What are you seeking?" and "Come with Me, and your eyes and heart will be opened, and you will see and understand."

The "tenth hour" in Hebrew time is around 4:00 P.M. or in Roman time it was 10:00 A.M. This moment was so significant for John that he records the actual time that he surrendered to Christ. Do you remember when you were first encountered the Savior? Do you remember the moment you believed?

Got to Tell Somebody

"One of the two which heard John speak, and followed him, was Andrew, Simon Peter's brother. He first findeth his own brother Simon, and saith unto him, We have found the Messias, which is, being interpreted, the Christ. And he brought him to Jesus" (John 1:40–42a).

"We look first at how Peter was drawn to Jesus. One can picture Andrew and John hurrying away from this momentous meeting. Andrew is saying, 'I must tell Simon.' John is saying, 'I'm going to get James. I've got to tell somebody.' 'He first found his own brother' can legitimately be rephrased, 'Andrew found first his own brother.' The implication is that Andrew found his brother first, that is, before John found his brother.

23. Morgan, Gospel According to John, 43.

THE BIRTH OF GOD

"It is well within the meaning of the text that both Andrew and John brought a brother to Jesus but that Andrew was first to do so. 'And he brought him to Jesus,' John says. This is characteristic of John telling us about Andrew's convert rather than his own. Andrew's convert became the first messenger of the church, Peter (Acts 2); John's convert, James, became the first martyr among the apostles."[24]

Never the Same

"And when Jesus beheld him, He said, Thou art Simon the son of Jona: thou shalt be called Cephas, which is by interpretation, A stone" (John 1:42b).

"You will be called Cephas" was a description of Peter's personality. Simon, or Simeon, was the name of Jacob's second oldest son (Genesis 29:33), who, with his brother Levi, had brutally avenged the defilement of their sister by a Canaanite prince. The brutish and impulsive propensity of Simeon was echoed in Simon. This characteristic is recorded for us in all the Gospels, as we can clearly see his reckless temper manifested (John 18:10).

The name Cephas is an Aramaic name. Peter is the Greek name. Both mean rock or stone. Jesus was saying "Simon, you can become Cephas or Peter if you follow me." The Gospels and history confirm the growth and development of the apostle. Peter was someone you could not depend on. He was unpredictable. Nevertheless, the Lord's eyes gazed deeply, piercing the eyes of Simon's. Simon could not escape, the Lord captured him. Although Simon Peter almost fell away, he never did. The principle is clear. When we follow Jesus, we change for the better. We are never the same.

Verses 43–44: "The day following Jesus would go forth into Galilee, and findeth Philip, and saith unto him, Follow me. Now Philip was of Bethsaida, the city of Andrew and Peter."

The Fourth Day

"The following day"—Day 1: Delegation came; Day 2: John's declaration; Day 3: Andrew, John, Peter; and now, it is day four.

"He found Philip." Notice the different methods of evangelism used:

24. Phillips, *Exploring John*, 44–45.

1. The approach used for Andrew and John was "mass evangelism." The message was Jesus is the Lamb of God. They heard the message, and they followed Christ.

2. Peter's conversion was a result of "personal evangelism" when Andrew found him and stated, "We have found the Messiah," and brought Peter to Jesus.

3. Philip's conversion was a result of "cold-contact evangelism." Jesus confronted Philip on the street. No one really attempted to witness to Philip. Jesus found him. This is a profound truth. Jesus finds us.

"We love Him, because He first loved us" (1 John 4:19).

"Follow Me"

This is the first time, as far as the record tells us, that Jesus uttered this formula He so loved to use. "Follow Me" or "Come and travel with Me" or "Come and journey with Me." Perhaps Jesus put His arm around Philip or on his shoulder with sincerity in His voice and, probably with a smile, said "Come with Me."

We are on an adventure with Jesus, a journey that embraces challenge, trial, rejection from the world, tribulation, sacrifice, and denial. But you will also find meaning, purpose of life, and ultimately fulfillment and peace, and above all eternal life with God through Christ.

Bethsaida, a town near the Sea of Galilee, means "house of fishing" and was home to Andrew and Peter.

See For Yourself

Verse 45: "Philip findeth Nathanael, and saith unto him, We have found him, of whom Moses in the law, and the prophets, did write, Jesus of Nazareth, the son of Joseph."

Philip with great enthusiasm found his friend Nathanael. His method of evangelism resembled Andrew's, perhaps with more emphasis using Scripture.

Nathanael was a student of the Hebrew Scriptures. He knew the Messiah would be born in Bethlehem. He poured over the prophecies. He knew the requirements. He was astonished at his friends enthusiasm about Jesus of Nazareth, the son of Joseph. Notice his response: "And Nathanael said unto him, Can there any good thing come out of Nazareth? Philip saith unto him, Come and see" (verse 46).

Nathanael came from Cana of Galilee (John 21:2), less than five miles from Nazareth. There was great prejudice against the little town of Nazareth. It was a backwoods town with a mixture of Gentile and Jewish residents. It had a poor reputation of being unsophisticated.

Because of "the coarseness of its dialect, the people from Judea held Galilee in low esteem. Jesus had an accent. Nathanael perhaps hedging for a time. Jesus, the Messiah? The son of Joseph? Surely not. From Nazareth? Impossible! Nazareth, in the Gospels, lived up to its reputation. It was the first city to greet Jesus's claims with violence and was ready to put Him to death on the strength of just one day's exposure to His teaching. He was actively hindered in ministry there because of the town's scornful rejection of His claims."[25]

Philip said, "Come and see for yourself . . . "

Finding God

Verses 47–48: "Jesus saw Nathanael coming to him, and saith of him, Behold an Israelite indeed, in whom is no guile! Nathanael saith unto him, Whence knowest thou me? Jesus answered and said unto him, Before that Philip called thee, when thou wast under the fig tree, I saw thee."

The Lord saw into Nathanael's soul. Speaking not to Nathanael, but to the others, he said,"Behold an Israelite indeed, in whom is no guile" (or deceit). Guile can be translated as he is not like Jacob. Jacob was a man of deceit in his early years, until God broke him physically and spiritually at Jabbok and changed him into Israel.

"After fleeing his uncle Laban's house, Jacob learns that his brother Esau is marching toward him (with 400 troops). Jacob is very frightened. Jacob cannot forget that when they last saw each other, Esau was plotting to murder him in revenge for Jacob's having deceptively procured from Isaac the blessing intended for Esau. That night while sleeping, Jacob is attacked by a man . . . and wrestled with him all night . . . Although (this man) is other-worldly (and) wounds him in the thigh, Jacob ultimately succeeds in pinning the man, refusing to free him until he gives him a blessing. The man awards Jacob with the additional name of Israel (Yisra'el) meaning 'you

25. Phillips, *Exploring John*, 47.

have wrestled with God and with men and prevailed.' The Jewish people, descendants from Jacob's twelve sons . . . eventually become known as B'nai Yisra'el, the children of Israel."[26]

Nathanael said, "How do you know me?" He agreed with the Lord's evaluation of his character. Nathanael was astounded as to how the Lord knew him.

"Before"—Simply before I knew you . . . before the foundation of the world I knew you.

"Under the fig tree I saw you"—This phrase is found in rabbinic literature and is used in the context of meditation on the Law. Students of Scripture would try to find a quiet place to study and meditate. The Lord's words imply that Jesus knew what Nathanael was thinking about, what he was meditating on. He was thinking about Jacob and the Genesis story of Jacob's ladder, the night Jacob was converted.

> "And Jacob went out from Beersheba, and went toward Haran. And he lighted upon a certain place, and tarried there all night, because the sun was set; and he took of the stones of that place, and put them for his pillows, and lay down in that place to sleep. And he dreamed, and behold a ladder set up on the earth, and the top of it reached to heaven: and behold the angels of God ascending and descending on it. And, behold, the Lord stood above it, and said, I am the Lord God of Abraham thy father, and the God of Isaac: the land whereon thou liest, to thee will I give it, and to thy seed; And thy seed shall be as the dust of the earth, and thou shalt spread abroad to the west, and to the east, and to the north, and to the south: and in thee and in thy seed shall all the families of the earth be blessed. And, behold, I am with thee, and will keep thee in all places whither thou goest, and will bring thee again into this land; for I will not leave thee, until I have done that which I have spoken to thee of. And Jacob awaked out of his sleep, and he said, Surely the Lord is in this place; and I knew it not. And he was afraid, and said, How dreadful is this place! this is none other but the house of God, and this is the gate of heaven. And Jacob rose up early in the morning, and took the stone that he had put for his pillows, and set it up for a pillar, and poured oil upon the top of it. And he called the name of that place Bethel: but the name of that city was called Luz at the first. And Jacob vowed a vow, saying, If God will be with me, and will keep me in this way that I go, and will give me bread to eat, and raiment to put on,

26. Telushkin, *Jewish Literacy*, 39–40.

So that I come again to my father's house in peace; then shall the Lord be my God: And this stone, which I have set for a pillar, shall be God's house: and of all that thou shalt give me I will surely give the tenth unto thee" (Gen. 28:10–22).

David very wisely counseled his son, Solomon, concerning God: "If you seek Him, He will let you find Him . . . " (1 Chron. 28:9).

This is what Nathanael was doing. This was true for Nathanael, and it can be true for you. You seek Christ and you will find Him.

"Jacob was filled with guile (deceit) and had been forced to leave home because he had lied to his father and swindled his brother. If under these circumstances Jacob was eligible for a revelation from God, would not Nathanael be even more worthy of such a blessing? Jesus said that Nathanael was free from deceit and used the imagery of Jacob's dream to describe the greater revelation He would give to Nathanael . . . Jesus implied that He Himself would be the medium of that revelation, and His order of the angel's procedure implies that they rose from earth to heaven with their inquiries and then returned to earth with the answers. The Lord's mission is to answer human need and to make sure that the answers are proclaimed."[27]

The fig tree is also usually a symbol of Israel as a nation in a fruitless state of unbelief under the old covenant. Nathanael represents part of the godly remnant in the nation who will come into the blessing of the new covenant by faith in Messiah Jesus.

Amen, Amen!

Verses 49–51: "Nathanael answered and saith unto him, Rabbi, thou art the Son of God; thou art the King of Israel. Jesus answered and said unto him, Because I said unto thee, I saw thee under the fig tree, believest thou? Thou shalt see greater things than these. And he saith unto him, Verily, verily, I say unto you, Hereafter ye shall see heaven open, and the angels of God ascending and descending upon the Son of man."

In verse 51, Jesus used the words "verily, verily" or most assuredly. These words can also be interpreted as meaning truly, truly or Amen, Amen (Hebrew *Amane*). The word "Amen" is a Hebrew word with roots in the ordinary Hebrew for belief, faithfulness, and truth. It is found closing the first book of Psalms: 'Amen and Amen' (Ps. 41:13) . . . The double 'Amen' is used for

27. Gaebelein, *Expositor's Bible*, 41.

solemn emphasis, to express the assurance that the prayer embodied in this doxology psalm would be answered. The same 'Amen, and Amen' closes the second book of Psalm 72:19 and also the third book (Ps. 89:52). The fourth book ends with a single 'Amen' and then, 'Praise ye the Lord' (Ps. 106:48). The final book of Psalms ends with five psalms each beginning and ending with another great Hebrew word, 'Hallelujah,' 'Praise ye the Lord.'

"It is interesting that John records the word 'Amen' in the apocalypse as a name of Christ (Rev. 1:18; 3:14). It is the name by which He addressed Himself to the lukewarm, end-time, Laodicean church. The word 'Amen' is also the last word in the Bible. The last thing God has to say to us is to leave us pondering a word that is a name for his beloved Son:

'The grace of our Lord Jesus Christ be with you all. Amen" (Rev. 22:21).

"Thus grace and truth did indeed come by Jesus Christ and, after affirming that, God has no more to say. The double 'Amen,' is used to emphasize the Lord's divine authority to mark the importance of what He was about to say, and to affirm the certainty of the truth He declared."[28]

Ladders and Angels

The double "amen" got Nathanael's attention. It reminded him of Jacob's conversion and the ladder with the angels ascending and descending from heaven to earth. Jesus was saying, "Nathanael, I am the ladder that links heaven and earth, God and man. I am the way to heaven. You have called me the Son of God. I am! You have called me the King of Israel. I am! I am the only way to God. The angels ascend and descend in celebration of me."

Notice the angels are ascending and descending, not descending and ascending. They are already here. They are stationed in every corner, every state, every country, everywhere people are located. Satan can't do anything about them. They are here for various reasons and they are in constant communication with heaven's command.

There are guardian angels who watch over children. Jesus said, "Take heed that ye despise not one of these little ones; for I say unto you, that in heaven their angels do always behold the face of My Father which is in heaven" (Matt. 18:10). These angels ascend this glorious stairway, heavily burdened, reporting before a holy God, cases of child abuse, neglect, rejection, and abortion. Then they descend with their new orders from their

28. Phillips, Exploring John, 48–49.

commander and chief to care for the little ones assigned to them, to watch over, and to protect and defend.

There are angels who are assigned to God's own people, over churches. Some reports are not good. But, thankfully, there are good reports of faithfulness and revival. Do you ever wonder what they report about you?

Who is Jesus?

The phrase "Son of Man" has varying levels of emphasis. One of which is a title for the millennial kingdom in which the Son of Man will sit on the throne in Jerusalem as King of Israel. There will be open communication between the heavenly Jerusalem and the earthly. Jesus is the glory of both.

"The title 'Son of Man' appears twelve times in the Gospel of John . . . As the 'Son of man' Jesus reveals divine truth (John 1:51); He has a supernatural origin (John 3:13; 6:62); His death by being 'lifted up' achieves salvation for men (John 3:14; 8:28; 12:34); He exercises the prerogative of final judgment (John 5:27); and He provides spiritual nourishment (John 6:27).

This title is also used of His being glorified (John 12:23; 13:31), which John applies specifically to death and resurrection (John 7:39; 12:16) . . .

In its general usage, it is the title of the incarnate Christ who is the representative of humanity before God and the representative of deity in human life. In the perfection of Christ's humanity, God finds the fullness of His expression to men."[29]

"And he is before all things, and by him all things consist" (Col. 1:17).

"For it pleased the Father that in him should all fullness dwell" (Col. 1:19).

"For in him dwelleth all the fullness of the Godhead bodily. And ye are complete in him, which is the head of all principality and power" (Col. 2:9–10).

"Christ is all, and in all" (Col. 3:11b).

The Son of Man, being Jacob's ladder, is God's link with earth.

"I saw in the night visions, and, behold, one like the Son of man came with the clouds of heaven, and came to the Ancient of days, and they brought him near before him" (Dan. 7:13).

---

29. Gaebelein, Expositor's Bible, 141.

"Jesus saith unto him, Thou hast said: nevertheless I say unto you, Hereafter shall ye see the Son of man sitting on the right hand of power, and coming in the clouds of heaven" (Matt. 26:64).

Are you connected with Him? Do you believe? Are you traveling with Him? Are you His disciple? Or are you still waffling in decision? Respond today.

Without Christ, you have no hope. He is our link to God and to eternal life.

What do you seek? What are you seeking? What are you seeking in life?

Jesus said, "Follow Me" or come and travel with Me or come and journey with Me. He is the Son of man. He is all and in all. He is all you need. You can be complete in Him! He is our fortress and strength. He is life itself.

—— Chapter 7 ——

Childhood of Jesus

Dedicated to Hyman Appelman—a faithful erudite of Scripture. It was through his powerful teaching I came to faith in Jesus the Messiah. To Zola Levitt whose influence on my life regarding the Jewish Roots of Christianity was nothing less than profound. Both men are in Heaven—I look forward to seeing Hyman once again and to meet Zola face-to-face for the first time on that great reunion day!

Preface

"Childhood of Jesus" looks at the life of Jesus's childhood from a Jewish perspective. This chapter discloses daily activities and interactions with family and friends of Jesus. What type of education did Jesus receive? What was expected of Jesus as a little boy? Did he know he was the Messiah? Did he perform miracles? How did the community respond to Mary's pregnancy? What would it be like to live 2,000 years ago? "Childhood of Jesus" pulls back the covers and exposes the cultural mores of the time of Messiah's childhood. This chapter is a guide to use in personal Bible study or in Bible groups, as well for the classroom or pulpit.

Anselm of Canterbury (c. 1033–1109) commented regarding the virgin-birth of the Messiah:

> "Exercise your pictorial art, then, not on an empty fiction, but upon a solid truth, and say that it is extremely fitting that, as the sin of man and the cause of our condemnation took their origin from a woman, so the cure for sin and the cause of our salvation must be born of a woman. And so that women may not despair of attaining to the lot of the blessed, because such great evil has issued from a woman, it was fitting that such a great good should issue from a woman, to revitalize their hope. Add this to your painting:

if it was a virgin who was the cause of all evil to the human race, it is far more fitting that it be a virgin who will be the cause of all good. Depict this also: if the woman whom God made from a man without a woman was made from a virgin, it is also extremely fitting that the man who will originate from a woman without a man be born of a virgin. But for the present let these examples suffice of the pictures that can be depicted on the fact that the God-man must be born of a virgin woman."[1]

Not much is recorded for us in the New Testament about the life of Jesus between his birth and the scene where He is in the temple talking with the scholars. Nor is there much written about His life between His time in the temple and the beginning of His ministry at the age of thirty. What was He doing during those "silent years"?

As we look at the record, according to Scripture, of the Lord's life and teaching, we find a Jewish cultural distinctive. We find a deep commitment to the Jewish customs and beliefs of His day. Jesus grew up in a Jewish family setting. His parents observed Jewish law and religious practices. Jesus would have celebrated all the Jewish holidays. He would have been faithful in observing the Sabbath, regularly attending synagogue as well as being exposed to rabbinical teaching and expectations. (Matt. 1; Luke 2; Luke 4)

Some believe that Jesus was not educated due to a few verses such as: "Can any good thing come out of Nazareth? And they were all amazed and marveled, saying . . . are not all these which speak Galileans? And the (religious) Jews marveled saying, how does this Man know letters, having never studied?" (John 1:46; Acts 2:7; John 7:17). These statements reflected a tension and bias between Judea and Galilee. Those in Judea saw themselves as being sophisticated and cultured. They saw the Galileans as being unsophisticated and uncultured. When a Judean heard a Galilean speak, they heard an accent that was very distinct and coarse.

Shmuel Safrai, Hebrew University Professor of Jewish History of the Mishnaic and Talmudic Periods, stated, "Not only do the number of first century Galilean sages exceed the number of Judean sages, but the moral and ethical quality of their teaching is still considered more highly than that of their Judean counterparts." [2]

Galilee would have been the conservative religious and political bastion of Israel. Anticipation for the advent of Messiah was very high in this

---

1. *Classics Devotional Bible*, 1176.
2. Bivin, *Dispatch*.

region. Now with this background in mind, let's consider Luke's account of Jesus's childhood in Luke 2:40–52 and draw some conclusions.

Family History

Luke 2:40–52

The Scripture does not record for us exactly what Jesus did between the age of twelve and the beginning of his public ministry at the age of thirty; however, John does tell us that "the world itself could not contain the books that would be written" about the Lord's life (John 21:25).

There are apocryphal writings, extra-biblical attempts to record so-called events in the life of Jesus. Stories include Jesus traveling to India studying yoga; Jesus, as a little boy in Egypt, making clay pigeons, touching them, and causing them to fly; plus, Jesus having an encounter with E.T.

The New Testament records for us that people knew Jesus, where He lived, and who His parents were (Matt. 13:55; Mark 6:3). Jesus grew up in a typical Jewish home, the son of a carpenter.

Shortly, after Jesus was born, Joseph took Mary and two-year-old Jesus to Egypt, because Herod ordered the children in Bethlehem slaughtered. Early Christians believed this was a fulfillment of Rachel weeping for her children (Jer. 31:15). How long the family lived in Egypt, we do not know; however, we do know that, when they came back, they settled in Nazareth (Matt. 2:19–23).

Luke records for us a brief sketch in the life of Jesus as a child being twelve years old (Luke 2:40)—"And the Child grew and became strong in spirit, filled with wisdom; and the grace of God was upon Him." The word grew (Gr. *Auxano*) is a term that implies a physical growth. The Hebrew equivalents are "tsemach," meaning a tender shoot or plant, or "gadel" which means becoming great. *Child* means half-grown boy or girl. Luke was simply telling us that Jesus grew up like any other little Jewish boy with no great responsibility except to parental and religious authority.

Luke continues and states in 2:52, "And Jesus increased in wisdom and stature, and in favor with God and men." The word *increased* means to be fruitful, to drive forward (through discipline), to advance. Within the context of verse 40, we have the description of Jesus growing up as a child before the age of twelve. Arriving at verse 52, we find a description of

Jesus as an adolescent through adulthood growing (increasing) mentally, physically, and spiritually.

Luke reveals events that occurred between Christ's birth and adolescence in verses 41–46—

> "His parents went to Jerusalem every year at the Feast of the Passover. And when He was twelve years old, they went up to Jerusalem according to the custom of the feast. When they had finished the days, as they returned, the boy Jesus lingered behind in Jerusalem. And Joseph and His mother did not know it; but supposing Him to have been in the company, they went a day's journey, and sought Him among their relatives and acquaintances. So when they did not find Him they returned to Jerusalem, seeking Him. Now so it was that after three days they found Him in the temple, sitting in the midst of the teachers both listening to them and asking them questions."

Three days refer to traveling away from the city one day, traveling back to the city one day, and another day to find him. The questioning and answering is called "putting sh'eilot" and was an intense dialogue between twelve-year-old Jesus and some of the greatest minds of biblical Judaism. Some believe this was the prototype of what would eventually become the bar mitzvah.

Luke then records the reaction of the scholars regarding this little boy in verse 47, "And all who heard Him were astonished at His understanding and answers." These scholars were dazed at the treatise coming from this child. However, apparently this did not impress Mary and Joseph. "So when they saw Him, they were amazed; and His mother said to Him, 'Son, why have You done this to us? Look, your father and I have sought You anxiously'" (verse 48).

Normally a Jewish woman would never barge in, breaking up a conversation of the sages as boldly as Mary did. Nevertheless, she was a mother and her son was missing. Now He was found. Notice her words: "Son"—a mixture of anger, relief, fear, joy; "your father and I"—a typical response for parents in a crisis moment plus relief. As parents, Mary and Joseph were anxious over Jesus's safety as there would have been a great infusion of people in Jerusalem for the Passover. Some suggest over a million visitors would have traveled to Jerusalem. A little boy could get lost in such a crowd.

At this intense moment Luke records for us a theological conundrum, "And He said to them, Why did you seek Me: Did you not know that I must be about My Father's business?" (verse 49) In this stage of his life, what was His Father's will (referring to His heavenly Father, not Joseph)? An assumed answer is found in the next verse, "Then He went down with them and came to Nazareth, and was subject to them, but His mother kept all these things in her heart" (verse 51). Therefore, as a teenager, Jesus would have remained "subject" to His earthly parents.

For Luke to know all these details, according to tradition, suggests that Mary may have told him her story, thus Luke would have learned these facts firsthand from the mother of Jesus.

Basically, according to the text, we have a little Jewish boy, living in Nazareth, helping his father around the carpenter's shop, running errands, fetching water in Nazareth for Mary and playing. According to tradition, sometime in Jesus's late teens or early twenties, Joseph died which would have had a profound impact on the family economically, socially, and emotionally.

Homework for Jesus

Education would have been important to Joseph and Mary. Two-thousand years ago, Jewish parents would give their four- or five-year-old child a honey cake with Psalm 119:103 inscribed on it. "How sweet are Your words to my taste; sweeter than honey to my mouth." This would have been one of the child's first lessons on the goodness of the Word of God. It is sweet to the taste. It is good for you.

From the Mishnah (Avot 5:21) we read regarding the life stages of a Jewish child: "At five years of age, one is ready for the study of the written Torah, at ten years of age the study of the Oral Torah, at thirteen for bar mitzvah, at fifteen for the study of halachot (rabbinic legal decisions), at eighteen for marriage, at twenty for pursuing a vocation, at thirty for entering one's full vigor." Education was highly esteemed and valued in Jewish society. Josephus stated: "Above all we pride ourselves on the education of our children, and regard as the most essential task in life the observance of our laws and of the pious practices based thereupon, which we have inherited." –Against Apion, 60

A synagogue in the first century usually had its own school called either "Bet Sefer," which is an elementary school, or "Bet Midrash," a secondary school. Along with the children, adults would study the Scripture and tradition. The formal educational process ended at the age of thirteen where most of the young people would go to work. A few good students would continue with part-time studies and working a job part-time. A few exceptional students would leave home and study with a famous rabbi as their families supported them. The Apostle Paul, an exceptional student, experienced such an education with the famous teacher Gamaliel.

The Babylonian Talmud, Shabbat 30a states: "Study is one of the highest forms of worship." The Mishnah, Avot 2:12 states: "Discipline yourself to study Torah, for you do not acquire it by inheritance." These texts remind us of the Jews at Berea who "were more noble . . . and searched the scriptures daily, whether those things were so" (Acts 17:11). These sayings were probably the motivational impetus behinds Paul's statement: "Study to shew thyself approved unto God, a workman that needeth not to be ashamed, rightly dividing the Word of truth" (2 Tim. 2:15). Peter declared: "Giving all diligence, add to your faith, virtue, and to virtue knowledge" (2 Pet. 1:5).

To own a copy of the scriptures or a Torah Scroll would have been difficult for the common person at the time of Jesus as any copy would have been expensive to own. Therefore, few families had copies of the scrolls. As a result, a lot of memorization had to take place. Shmuel Safrai, stated: "There is the frequent expression, 'the chirping of children,' which was heard by people passing close by a synagogue as the children were reciting a verse. Adults too, in individual and group study, often read aloud; for it was frequently advised not to learn in a whisper, but aloud. This was the only way to overcome the danger of forgetting."[3]

The sages believed repetition was very important to learning. "A person who repeats his lesson a hundred times is not to be compared with him who repeats it a hundred and one times"—Babylonian Talmud, Hagigah 9b. "If (a student) learns Torah and does not go over it again and again, he is like a man who sows without reaping" –Babylonian Talmud, Sanhedrin 99a. If students memorized outdoors, they often could be distracted by the beautiful scenery, therefore, the Mishnah states: "A person walking along the road repeating his lessons who interrupts his memorization and exclaims: 'What a beautiful tree!' or 'What a beautiful field!' it is imputed to him as if he were guilty of a crime punishable by death" (Avot 3:8). Education, therefore, was very important to the first century family, and Jesus would have been exposed to the best possible training the family could muster.

3. *Jewish People*, 953.

We just covered the New Testament account of the childhood of Jesus, looked at early Christian thought about Jesus's birth, and briefly skimmed over early Hebraic impulses about Jewish life two-thousand years ago. Now, let's take it one step further and look at a mystical psalm that pulls back a curtain and allows us to peek at the Holy Family living in Nazareth.

Psalm 69: Mystical Words

Psalm 69 is a mystical and messianic psalm. Yes, David was writing of his personal experience and challenges, and yet he wrote of the woes of another yet to come. This psalm is one of the most quoted psalms in the New Testament as it refers to the Messiah. This poetic portrait is a presage to be sure, mysterious in context and mystical in expounding profound spiritual insights. It takes us behind the scenes, revealing the childhood of Messiah, the One who was foretold to come. We discover the personal pain Jesus experienced as a little boy, a precursor of things to come when he was an adult. The psalm was written approximately 900 years before Mary gave birth to her firstborn son. Let's take a look at this marvelous expose of the childhood of Jesus:

Verses 1–4: He didn't do it, however He must fix it

"Save me, O God! For the waters have come up to my neck. I sink in deep mire, where there is no standing; I have come into deep waters, where the floods overflow me. My throat is dry; My eyes fail while I wait for my God. Those who hate me without a cause are more than the hairs of my head; They are mighty who would destroy me, Being my enemies wrongfully; Though I have stolen nothing, I still must restore it."

These verses reveal to us one who is wrongfully accused with multitudes hating Him without cause. He must restore that which he did not take. These factors are clearly a reference to the cross and the redemption that comes through the shed blood of the Lamb, a restoring of the soul's relationship that has been severed because of sin. We also see an inference to the crying of a boy or a young child experiencing distress or anguish.

Verse 7: Suffering Lamb

"Because for Your sake I have borne reproach;
Shame has covered my face."

Verse seven is another clear reference to Messiah as the suffering Lamb of God—Jesus, the One who would stand before the officials of Jerusalem hearing the crowd's false accusations and experiencing the full thrust of Rome's judicial power. Jesus's teaching moved the masses and upset the religious order. That day in the place where the glory of God abode in the Holy of Holies, Jesus, the incarnate God, was about to endure history's most grueling punishment of all—the cross. He was innocent, yet He bore our reproach and shame.

Verses 8–9: Bastard Son

"I have become a stranger to my brothers, and an alien to my moth-
er's children; Because zeal for Your house has eaten me up, and the
reproaches of those who reproach You have fallen on me."

These verses speak of the rejection of Jesus by not only the religious leaders of his day, but also his disciples who fled from his side when the Roman soldiers, led by Judas, came to take Jesus away. And yet, there is another level of interpretation that references his siblings as he was growing up who did not believe until after the resurrection.

Nazareth was a little town of about two hundred people in the time of Jesus. The townspeople found it difficult to accept Jesus and to believe that He was the Son of God (Prov. 30:4; John 2:17; Luke 8:19; Rom. 15:3). There would have been a lot of gossip about Mary. The talk about town would have gone something like this, "Joseph was not the Father. They said it was an angel that appeared to her and announced she was pregnant. Can you believe it?"

This kind of talk would have been emphasized in Mark 6:3 where Jesus taught in his hometown synagogue and the congregants who knew Jesus made these comments: "Is this not the carpenter, the Son of Mary . . . ?" First of all, in Jewish culture a son was never identified through his mother, only through his father. Jesus should have been addressed as Yeshua ben Yossi or Jesus son of Joseph. By referencing him as Yeshua ben Mariam or son of Mary, they were calling him a bastard son, or directly insulting Mary as a loose woman of low morals. Jesus was simply not accepted in his home town and would have been considered a bastard son.

His younger siblings would have been affected by the peer pressure of the townspeople. There would have been an immeasurable amount of tension between family members and the community.

Verses 11–12: Ridiculed by Neighbors

"I also made sackcloth my garment; I became a byword to them. Those who sit in the gate speak against me, and I am the song of the drunkards."

Sackcloth is a symbol of a servant and also associated with guilt. Jesus, being God-man, bore our guilt of sin on the cross. Some believe that sackcloth was used on the one crucified in order to fasten him more securely on the cross.

Jesus, growing up and being a citizen of Nazareth, would have been ridiculed by the neighbors to the point of becoming a slanderous byword, a proverb, at the places of important dialogue within the community. The elders, rulers, judges, or officials who sat at the gate of the city of Nazareth would have talked about Mary and Joseph and their "situation" with Jesus.

The drunkards may refer to those in Nazareth as he was growing up or to those in Jerusalem during the Passover celebration after drinking wine. Perhaps the psalmist was also referring to the soldiers who may have drunk the spiced wine used to dull the senses of those on the cross and substituted it with vinegar. Nevertheless, you get the picture.

Verses 19–21: Heavy Heart

"You know my reproach, my shame, and my dishonor; My adversaries are all before You. Reproach has broken my heart, and I am full of heaviness; I looked for someone to take pity, but there was none; And for comforters, but I found none. They also gave me gall for my food, and for my thirst they gave me vinegar to drink."

The Lord manifested compassion on those who hated him, who made fun of him, who made his name a byword from an early age. As a child his heart became so heavy looking for someone to take pity and found none. Moments like these would have prepared Jesus, as a small-town boy, for the eventual challenge of facing adversaries in the Roman courts, ultimately leading up to his execution in the years to come. While hanging on the cross between heaven and earth, dying for something he didn't do, he was able to say, "Father, forgive them for they know not what they do" (Luke 23:34).

Gall and vinegar are clear references to the cross as they attempted to give the Lord this gall (sedative, pain reliever) and sour wine to drink, but he refused it (Matt. 27:34, 48; Mark 15:23; Luke 23:36; John 19:29).

Verse 26: Smitten

"For they persecute him whom thou hast smitten; and they talk to the grief of those whom thou hast wounded."

We are reminded of the Isaiah's words about the Messiah and the reason for this prophetic chapter: Jesus "shall grow up . . . despised and rejected . . . a man of sorrows and acquainted with grief . . . persecuted, smitten of God and afflicted . . . Yet it pleased the Lord to bruise Him, He has put him to grief . . . He was numbered with the transgressors, and He bore the sin of many and made intercession for the transgressors" (53:3–5, 10, 12). Also, Zechariah stated, "Strike the shepherd, and the sheep will be scattered" (13:7).

We discover with the texts of the prophets that God orchestrated all the events regarding the life and childhood of Jesus leading up the death, burial, and resurrection.

So in the final analysis:

1. Jesus was imperiled at birth as Herod tried to kill him.

2. He was an alien in Egypt as a child.

3. He was made slanderous by word (made fun of) and gossiped about in his hometown.

4. He was misunderstood by his siblings and peers.

5. His mother was ridiculed with gossip from the town's people questioning her morals.

6. Jesus's earthly Father died at a most crucial time when a young man needs his dad.

7. As an adult, Jesus was rejected, abused, and ultimately crucified.

Why? Why would the infinite, eternal God go to such length to create human beings only to have them resist the One who gave them life? Why would the all-powerful God choose to reveal himself through the passage of a virgin's womb, becoming a little boy? Why would the all-knowing God want this manifestation of himself to become part of a tribe of people that is so misunderstood? Why would he subject himself to the brutality of a horrible execution? Why would God reveal his essence this way?

"Seeing then that we have a great High Priest who has passed through the heavens, Jesus the Son of God, let us hold fast our confession. For we do not have a High Priest who cannot sympathize with our weaknesses, but was in all points tempted as we are, yet without sin. Let us therefore come boldly to the throne of grace, that we may obtain mercy and find grace to help in time of need" (Heb. 4:14–16).

The infinite, eternal Son became flesh so we might understand. He experienced every human trial and testing. Therefore, he does understand our need! Will you give your burden over to the One who can help and come to the One who can give you hope, comfort, peace, and eternal life?

Time is short, life is precious, and Jesus is coming soon!

—— Chapter 8 ——

Metamorphosis Factor

Contact with Heaven, The Rehearsal

Matthew 17; Mark 9; Luke 9

"And after six days Jesus taketh Peter, James, and John his brother, and bringeth them up into an high mountain apart" (Matt. 17:1).

DURING THE LAST SIX months of the Lord's life on earth, between verses one and two of John 7, a most incredible episode took place. John first mentions the episode in John 1:14, " . . . We (Peter, James, and John) beheld his glory, the glory as of the only begotten of the Father,) full of grace and truth."

John 7:1 says, "After these things Jesus walked in Galilee: for he would not walk in Jewry, because the Jews sought to kill him." Because the tenses are all imperfect, a better rendering would be "After these things Jesus was walking in Galilee, for He did not desire to walk in Judaea, because the religious rulers sought to kill Him." Please take note in verse two that the Feast of the Tabernacles was at hand.

What was the episode that took place? The incredible event was the transfiguration when Jesus took his three choice disciples up to Mt. Hermon to pray.

Some believe this scene took place on Mt. Tabor. This is unlikely because there was a fortress on top of Tabor during the time of Christ. Mt. Hermon is 9,400 feet high and some 11,000 feet above the Jordan Valley and can be seen from the Dead Sea, which is more than 100 miles away. This would have been a most difficult climb, and the men would not have reached the summit. More than likely they were on one of the slopes as it was beginning to become nightfall. Some believe this was the evening after the Sabbath.

The panorama from Hermon would have been glorious. They would have seen part of Syria, Lebanon, the Jordan Valley, the Dead Sea, Galilee, Samaria, and Jerusalem. On a clear night, the stars would shine brilliantly in the sky. The moon would have cast shadows from the trees. Patches of glistening snow would be illuminated. The men were far from the religious polemic of the Scribes and Pharisees. Upon this mountain they stood between the Hebraic and Hellenistic cultural influences. And upon this mountain, Jesus prayed to His Father to verify whether this was the time for which He came.

Peter, James, and John were the Lord's most trusted men. He took them with Him, not only to Mt. Hermon, but also to the house of Jairus when Jesus healed his twelve-year-old daughter and to the Garden—"And when he came into the house, he suffered no man to go in, save Peter, and James, and John, and the father and the mother of the maiden" (Luke 8:51).

Into a High Mountain to Pray

> "And it came to pass about an eight days after these sayings, he took Peter and John and James, and went up into a mountain to pray" (Luke 9:28).

This reminds us of Abraham ascending Mt. Moriah with Isaac, testing their faith and affirming the truthfulness, holiness, and mercy of God as He provided the ram for sacrifice. It's also a reminder of Moses's ascent to Sinai where he entered the presence of God via the burning bush and then ultimately entered the shekinah glory, being the recipient of the Law among the thundering and light of the Creator's essence. It reminds us of Elijah receiving sustenance from an angel after a great victory on Carmel, running from Jezebel, ascending to Mt. Horeb (the same place Moses met with God in the Sinai), and hearing the still small voice of God, saying "Go on, Elijah, I have seven thousand who have not bowed down to Baal, who have not kissed him."

Now, Jesus comes to the mountain to seek His Father's will. After the ascent to Hermon, Luke records that Peter, James, and John were heavy with sleep. (They would also fall asleep in the Garden.) This is very natural after an arduous, steep climb up a mountain path. Exhausted, perhaps battling the thin mountain air, weakened by hunger and thirst, they fell asleep only to be awakened by a most glorious sight.

"But Peter and they that were with him were heavy with sleep: and when they were awake, they saw his glory, and the two men that stood with him" (Luke 9:32).

"What they saw was their Master, while praying, transformed. The 'form of God' shone through the 'form of a servant': the 'appearance of His Face became other,' 'it did shine as the sun' . . . the whole figure seemed bathed in light, the very garments whiter far than the snow on which the moon shone . . . 'flittering,' 'white as the light.'"[1]

Transfigured

"And was transfigured before them: and his face did shine as the sun, and his raiment was white as the light" (Matt. 17:2).

"And after six days Jesus taketh with him Peter, and James, and John, and leadeth them up into an high mountain apart by them-selves: and he was transfigured before them" (Mark 9:2).

The Greek *metemorphothe* gives us our English word *metamorphosis*. "A metamorphosis is a change on the outside that comes from the inside . . . Our Lord's glory was not reflected but radiated from within. There was a change on the outside that came from within as He allowed His essential glory to shine forth."[2]

"And as he prayed, the fashion of his countenance was altered, and his raiment was white and glistering" (Luke 9:29). Luke tells us "his countenance was altered" . . . which means Jesus "became other," "different," "strange," something quite unknown. The writer of Hebrews states that "The Son is the radiance of God's glory and the exact representation of His being" (Heb. 1:3 (NIV)).

Peter, James, and John were experiencing a glimpse of the very essence and glory of God the Father through God the Son. The very shekinah glory of Sinai and the *kodesh ha kodeshim* was in their presence.

What an affirmation of Peter's confession at Caeserea Phillipi at the base of Mt. Hermon when Jesus asked His disciples, "Whom do men say that I the Son of man am?" and Peter answered and said, "Thou art the

1. Edersheim, *Life and Times*, 96.
2. Wiersbe, *Be Loyal*, 117.

Christ, the Son of the living God" (Matt. 16:16). Peter confessed and then received assurance.

What happened to Peter is like Mary and Martha, whose brother Lazarus died. When Jesus arrived, they said, "Lord, if thou hadst been here, (our brother would not have died).

Jesus said, "I am the resurrection, and the life: he that believeth in me, though he were dead, yet shall he live: And whosoever liveth and believeth in me shall never die. Believest thou this?" (John 11:25–26)

They believed and rolled away the stone, and Jesus said, "Lazarus, come forth . . . loose him, and let him go!"

Elijah and Moses

> "And, behold, there talked with him two men, which were Moses and Elias" (Luke 9:30).

It was quite fitting for these two pillars of the Old Testament to appear with Jesus. First of all, both Moses and Elijah had unique obituaries written about them. Deuteronomy tells of the mysterious death of Moses on Mount Nebo overlooking the Dead Sea, Jericho, and the Promised Land. The Scriptures gives us the impression that God Himself buried the Great Giver of the Law. Elijah's departure in a chariot and horses of fire was nothing less than awesome as Elisha, his disciple, beheld his ascension into the heavens.

Jewish scholars teach that Moses is to accompany the Messiah and be His consort. And Elijah is to call the people of Israel back to God and prepare the way for, and herald the coming of, the Messiah and the Messianic Kingdom.

Moses was the greatest of the law-givers, and Elijah was the greatest prophet. "These two men were the twin peaks of Israel's religious history and achievement."[3] They were the foundation of the Law and the pillar of the prophets. "In them all history rose up and pointed Jesus on His way. In them all history recognized Jesus as its own consummation."[4]

3. Barclay, *Matthew*, 176.
4. Barclay, *Matthew*, 177.

The Conversation

"Who appeared in glory, and spake of his decease which he should accomplish at Jerusalem" (Luke 9:3).

There are two Greek words translated "decease or deceased."

1. *Teleutao* (tel-yoo-taht-o): to decease or to end life (Matt. 22:25).

2. *Exodus*: out-going (Luke 9:31). Peter uses the same word referencing his own "out-going," in the context of describing the transfiguration (2 Pet. 1:15). To understand *exodus* or out-going, we must contrast Luke's antonym describing the Lord's "in-coming."

"When John had first preached before his coming the baptism of repentance to all the people of Israel" (Acts 13:24).

Eisodos (icé-od-us) means entrance, into, of place, time or purpose, a road or journey. Paul, speaking at a synagogue in Antioch in Pisidia, gave a synopsis of the anticipation of the "in-coming" or entrance of the Messiah. He talked about the Exodus, Judges, Prophets, David's seed from which Messiah would come, and John the Baptist preaching "before his eisodos" (coming) or before Messiah's purposed journey began.

Now, on Mt. Hermon, we have a dialogue concerning the Messiah's exodus, His "out-going," and ending His purposed journey, which embraces not only His death, but its method, resurrection, and ascension. This "He should accomplish at Jerusalem." *Accomplish* or *Pleroo* (play-ró-o) means to make full, fill out, to fulfill, perfect.

So, the dialogue that was on the lips of Moses and Elijah was relative to Jesus fulfilling the Law, fulfilling the prophecies, types, and shadows. What a holy, eternal moment these precious disciples observed. This experience became paramount for these three disciples. It was good for these men to have witnessed a glimpse of the future glory which was theirs and is for all who trust in Christ alone.

This became a motivational impetus for them as James became the first apostle to be martyred by Herod's hand of hatred. Herod hated him because James was tenacious like the Rock of Gibraltar. Peter, the most human of the apostles, ultimately stood gloriously for Christ even unto death as he was crucified, upside down. And John, who was imprisoned, boiled in oil, and exiled to Patmos, was the last apostle to die. They remembered Mt. Hermon and, therefore, did not fear their "out-going," their exodus, the end of their journey.

Three Tabernacles

"And it came to pass, as they departed from him, Peter said unto Jesus, Master, it is good for us to be here: and let us make three tabernacles; one for thee, and one for Moses, and one for Elias: not knowing what he said" (Luke 9:33).

Peter saw this event in connection with the Feast of Tabernacles, also called Feast of Booths or Succoth. Succoth is celebrated each year in the Autumn, reminding Jewish people of the exodus and how the Israelites lived in booths or tents (temporary dwellings) until the younger generation was allowed to enter the Promised Land. It also looked forward to Israel's full blessings from God when He gathers His people into the land in the last days. The Feast of Tabernacles points to the Messiah's reign on earth, the millennial kingdom.

Mark tells us that Peter did not know what to say, because they were terrified. "For he wist not what to say; for they were sore afraid" (Mark 9:6). Peter had the right idea, but the wrong time. "While he thus spake, there came a cloud, and overshadowed them: and they feared as they entered into the cloud" (Luke 9:34).

"A strange peculiarity has been noticed about Hermon in 'the extreme rapidity of the formation of the clouds on the summit . . . In a few minutes a thick cap forms over the top of the mountain, and as quickly disperses and entirely disappears.'"[5] Suddenly, this cloud appears on the brow of the mountain. A very unusual cloud. A cloud that is illuminated, full of light that "overshadowed" them:

"While he yet spake, behold, a bright cloud overshadowed them: and behold a voice out of the cloud, which said, this is my beloved Son, in whom I am well pleased; hear ye him" (Matt. 17:5).

"And there was a cloud that overshadowed them: and a voice came out of the cloud, saying, this is my beloved Son: hear him" (Mark 9:7).

Overshadowed means to cast a shadow upon, to envelope or enwrap in a haze of brilliancy. "As it laid itself between Jesus and the two Old Testament representatives, it parted, and presently enwrapped them."[6] This was

---

5. Edersheim, *Life and Times*, 97.
6. Edersheim, *Life and Times*, 97.

nothing less than the very "presence of God, revealing, yet concealing—a cloud, yet luminous."[7]

Terror apprehended the disciples as the fringe and shadow of this glorious cloud touched them. This was the same cloud that permeated Israel's history. This cloud led the people during the exodus and wilderness wanderings (Exod. 13:21–22). It covered the tabernacle at its completion (Exod. 40:34). And it filled the house of the Lord at the dedication of Solomon's Temple (1 Kings 8:10, 11; 2 Chron. 5:13, 7:2). Perhaps, most memorable is when this divine glory, the shekinah, came down upon Mount Sinai on the very top of the mountain. Let's read . . .

> "And Moses brought forth the people out of the camp to meet with God; and they stood at the nether part of the mount. And Mount Sinai was altogether on a smoke, because the Lord descended upon it in fire: and the smoke thereof ascended as the smoke of a furnace, and the whole mount quaked greatly" (Exod. 19:17–18).

In Jewish thought, when the Lord descended upon the mount, "when He began to lower His shekinah. At this point, the mountain shook and rose to meet Him, as a servant runs to greet his master . . . the activity of the mountain: though inanimate, became alive."[8] The whole earth groans for the glory of God. "For we know that the whole creation groaneth and travaileth in pain together until now" (Rom. 8:22).

All inanimate images and gods will bow down before Him. "Confounded be all they that serve graven images, that boast themselves of idols: worship him, all ye gods" (Psalm 97:7).

A Voice

"While he yet spake, behold, a bright cloud overshadowed them: and behold a voice out of the cloud, which said, this is my beloved Son, in whom I am well pleased; hear ye him" (Matt. 17:5).

"Hear ye Him . . . "

To the Jew this cloud represented the very presence of God, the shekinah. There was no mistake as to what was taking place, and it is as though Matthew was astounded as to what he was writing as he said, "Behold" (verses 3, 5).

---

7. Edersheim, *Life and Times*, 97.

8. Agnon, *Present at Sinai*, 186.

"And, behold, there appeared unto them Moses
and Elias talking with him" (Matt. 17:3).

Pause, and look at this. Please know what is taking place!

Behold, Moses and Elijah . . . Behold, the bright cloud . . . Behold, the voice out of the cloud . . . This voice was a confirmation for Jesus that this was the hour for which He came. It was also a confirmation for the disciples and for us. He is " . . . all and in all" (Col. 3:11). "Ye are complete in Him . . . " (Col. 2:10). "He is before all things, and by him all things consist" (Col. 1:17). He is truth, the totality of truth (John 14:6).

> "And when the disciples heard it, they fell on their face, and were
> sore afraid. And Jesus came and touched them, and said, Arise,
> and be not afraid. And when they had lifted up their eyes, they saw
> no man, save Jesus only" (Matt. 17:6–8).

As Isaiah trembled in the presence of the Lord and cried out, "Woe is me! For I am undone; because I am a man of unclean lips . . . for mine eyes have seen the King, the Lord of hosts" (Isa. 6:5) and as John will once again fall prostrate before a glorified Lord on the isle of Patmos, Peter, James, and John fall "on their face and were sore afraid."

Touched (Greek *Haptomai* (hap'-tom-ahee) means to hold on, fasten to, embrace, to set on fire.

Verse 8: They saw no one but Jesus. Who do you see? Who do you look upon? Christ is all we need!

John made reference to the transfiguration when he stated, "And the Word was made flesh, and dwelt among us (and we beheld His glory, the glory as of the only begotten of the Father), full of grace and truth" (John 1:14).

And Peter recalls his experience on the Mount of Transfiguration where he saw the Lord unveiled in glory. This same glory that will be seen at His coming.

> "Knowing that shortly I must put off this my tabernacle, even as
> our Lord Jesus Christ hath shewed me. Moreover I will endeav-
> our that ye may be able after my decease to have these things
> always in remembrance. For we have not followed cunningly
> devised fables, when we made known unto you the power and
> coming of our Lord Jesus Christ, but were eyewitnesses of his
> majesty. For he received from God the Father honour and glory,
> when there came such a voice to him from the excellent glory,
> This is my beloved Son, in whom I am well pleased. And this

voice which came from heaven we heard, when we were with him in the holy mount" (2 Pet. 1:14–18).

NIV study notes for 2 Peter 1:16 state, "In Christ's transfiguration the disciples received a foretaste of what His coming will be like when He returns to establish His eternal kingdom." This was a "rehearsal" of the Second Coming.

There should be no chapter division between Matthew 16:28 and 17:1.

"After six days . . ." (Matt. 17:1). "It appears that these six days hark back to Exodus 24:16–18 and are intended to parallel the theophany at Sinai."[9]

> "And the glory of the Lord abode upon Mount Sinai, and the cloud covered it six days: and the seventh day he called unto Moses out of the midst of the cloud. And the sight of the glory of the Lord was like devouring fire on the top of the mount in the eyes of the children of Israel. And Moses went into the midst of the cloud, and gat him up into the mount: and Moses was in the mount forty days and forty nights" (Exod. 24:16–18).

> "For the Son of man shall come in the glory of His Father, with His angels . . . " (Matt. 16:27).

> "[T]he Son of man shall come in His glory, and all the holy angels with Him, then shall He sit upon the throne of His glory, and before Him shall be gathered all nations . . . " (Matt. 25:31–32).

> "Looking for that blessed hope, and the glorious appearing of the great God and our Saviour Jesus Christ" (Titus 2:13).

> "Behold, He cometh with clouds; and every eye shall see Him . . . " (Rev. 1:7).

John warns us, "And now, little children, abide in Him; that, when He shall appear, we may have confidence, and not be ashamed before Him at His coming" (1 John 2:28).

Verse 9: They came down from the mountain

At this point, Jesus begins to conclude His public ministry heading toward the cross, the grave, and Resurrection Sunday.

What conclusions can we draw from this transfiguration experience?

9. Lach, *Rabbinic Commentary*, 259.

1. "Jesus laid aside His glory when He came to earth. Because of the finished work on the cross, He not only received back His glory, but now shares it with us who believe."[10]

    "And now, O Father, glorify thou me with thine own self with the glory which I had with thee before the world was. . . . And the glory which thou gavest me I have given them; that they may be one, even as we are one: . . . Father, I will that they also, whom thou hast given me, be with me where I am; that they may behold my glory, which thou hast given me: for thou lovedst me before the foundation of the world" (John 17:5, 22, 24).

2. We need not fear the future nor the mystery of death.

    "There is a most comforting lesson for us in the fact that the disciples knew Moses and Elijah. We will not have to be introduced when we get to heaven but '. . . then shall I know even as also I am known' (1 Cor. 13:12). Likewise, the heavenly visitors knew what was transpiring on earth and of the coming crucifixion of the Saviour . . . Our loved ones who have gone on before know what is transpiring on earth. They cannot speak to us but they are a great cloud of witnesses about us (Hebrews 12:1). They rejoice in the presence of the angels when a sinner repents.

    "I say unto you, that likewise joy shall be in heaven over one sinner that repenteth, more than over ninety and nine just persons, which need no repentance. . . . Likewise, I say unto you, there is joy in the presence of the angels of God over one sinner that repenteth" (Luke 15:7, 10).

    The unseen world is not far away and how happy are they who are with the Saviour there."[11]

3. Because of this "rehearsal" or glimpse of our future glory, we have hope.

    "Behold, what manner of love the Father hath bestowed upon us, that we should be called the sons of God: therefore the world knoweth us not, because it knew him not. Beloved, now are we the sons of God, and it doth not yet appear what we shall be: but we know that, when

10. Wiersbe, *Be Loyal*, 117.

11. Rice, *King*, 260–61.

he shall appear, we shall be like him; for we shall see him as he is. And every man that hath this hope in him purifieth himself, even as he is pure" (1 John 1:1–3).

John was there . . . Rejoice, beloved, rejoice . . . In the hope of eternal glory that is ours for those in Christ. Do you see Christ only? Do you see Him?

Chapter 9

God's Passion: A Look at the Cross

The Cry

"Eli, Eli, lama sabachthani?" cried Jesus on the cross. "My God, my God, why have You forsaken me?" (Matt. 27:46).

AT THAT MOMENT, HEAVEN stood still in awe. A paradigm shift took place. Something changed. The angels had to marvel. The heavenly beings must have gasped. For the first time in eternity, God the Father turned His face from God the Son. Why would the Father turn His face? Why? What happened? Before I endeavor to answer that question, let's go back to the beginning.

John 1:1

"In the beginning was the Word, and the Word was with God, and the Word was God."

The opening verse in the Gospel of John reminds us of the opening verse in Genesis: "In the beginning God created the heaven and the earth." Genesis chapter one connects the Creator with the creation. Timeless eternity, non-time, before time, the eternal past, or preface to time is being referred to here. Before anything existed, God was there. Then He created.

John, in his opening statements, also connects the Creator with the creation. He uses the Greek word *"Logos,"* translated "Word." The way John uses "Logos" is to emphasize that the "Word" was the designer, genius, or the mind behind the creation of the universe.

Eternally God

John then says this Logos *"was God."* The Greek word translated "was" is in the imperfect tense which means it is something continuous. It doesn't refer to something that is past, present, or future, but rather, something that has no beginning or ending. It always has existed with no beginning and no ending, referencing that the Logos was the same, not "as" God, nor "a" God, but God Himself, with no beginning and no ending.

The Logos, writes John, "was made flesh and dwelt among us" (John 1:14). When John remarks about the "Word," he is speaking of Jesus. Jesus, John says, is God. Therefore, when we think of Jesus, we must think of Jesus as never having a beginning, nor never having an ending. He is eternally, equally, unquestionably God.

Face to Face

Notice in the middle of verse one of John 1:1: *"the Word was with God."* This little word translated "with" in the Greek is *"pros."* "Pros" means "Face to face," a sense of intimacy, interfacing, living intercourse, communion, fellowship, a similar nature or likeness, and a sense of home. All of this implies separate personality and yet complete union. This boggles the mind! Verse one of John is speaking of the union of the Godhead: Father, Son, and Holy Spirit, or, the Trinity.

Therefore, from the very beginning of eternity past, you had the Father and the Son having eternal co-existence and unity, and yet at the Cross of Calvary Jesus cried out, "My God, My God why hast thou forsaken me?" What happened?

Forsaken

The Scripture states that God cannot look upon iniquity (sin). "Thou art of purer eyes than to behold evil, and canst not look on iniquity" (Hab. 1:13). In fact, it is recorded many times that God will hide His face from sin, thus turning His face of fellowship and blessing. (Deut. 31:18; Ps. 44:24; Isa. 1:15; 59:2; 64:7; Ezek. 39:23; Mic. 3:4).

When Jesus hung on the cross, He became sin. Paul said in Galatians 3:13, "Christ has redeemed us from the curse of the law, having become a curse for us (for it is written, 'Cursed is everyone who hangs on a tree.')."

The Prophet Isaiah stated, "All we like sheep have gone astray; we have turned everyone to his own way; and the Lord has laid on Him (Messiah) the iniquity of us all" (53:6).

What does this mean? It means that when Jesus was hanging there on the cross, at that very moment when he cried, "My God, My God, why hast thou forsaken me?", He bore our sin, thus becoming sin (Isa. 53:12; Heb. 9:28; 1 Pet. 2:24; 1 John 3:5). He became murder, adultery, lying, lust, and everything you can think of regarding the nature of sin. Therefore, the union of fellowship that the Son had with the Father from the very beginning was severed. For the first time in all eternity, God the Father turned His face from God the Son. Jesus became sin (iniquity), therefore, the Father hid His face from Jesus who became sin for us. Jesus was paying the penalty for sin, so that those who believe and trust in Him alone for salvation will receive forgiveness and eternal life with God (John 3:16).

It Is Finished

Moments later, Jesus said, "It is finished! And bowing His head, He gave up His spirit" (John 19:30). Jesus died.

Do you remember when Jesus said, "I lay down my life that I may take it again. No man takes it from Me, but I lay it down of Myself. I have power to lay it down, and I have power to take it again" (John 10:17–18)? Jesus declared that nobody would kill him, but that He would choose where, how, and when to die.

Wait a minute! The soldiers nailed Jesus to the cross. Yes. However, Jesus chose the moment when He would die.

During this time of year, the Jews were getting ready for the Passover. It is said that approximately one million Jews from all over the known world would have come to Jerusalem to celebrate this holiday remembering the Jewish Exodus out of Egypt and all the miracles God manifested in Egypt and the wilderness.

Part of the tradition and celebration included the head of each household taking a lamb to the Temple to be slaughtered as a sacrifice unto the Lord. Each family would procure a lamb and tend to it making sure it was without spot or blemish.

Then at the appointed time on the day of Passover, the heads of the households, wearing a special white outer garment, would carry the lambs on their shoulders into the Temple. They would line up by the thousands.

At 3:00 P.M., the time of the afternoon sacrifice, a priest would climb to the top of the wall and blow the shofar (trumpet) indicating that it was time to offer the Passover lamb. The heads of the households would take a special sacrificial knife and slit the lamb's throat. Some of the lambs' blood would splatter on the white garments worn by the men. The priests, who were standing by, would catch the rest of the blood in a basin and then offer the blood upon the altar. The men would prepare the lamb and, still wearing their blood-stained garments, walk home to eat the lamb with family and friends. The blood-stained garment was horrifying to look at; it was a reminder of the payment for redemption from bondage and from sin.

Hearing the Trumpet

Jesus was on the cross for six hours during the time of Passover. He was nailed to the cross at the third hour (the Jewish first hour is 6 A.M.; therefore, the third hour would be 9 A.M.). He died on the cross at the ninth hour or 3 P.M. (Matt. 27:45; Mark 15:34; Luke 23:44).

Jesus, if he was positioned in the right direction, possibly could have seen part of the Temple. The Temple was a massive, majestic, beautiful edifice on the south side of Mount Moriah. This was the same location where Abraham bound Isaac (Gen. 22). The place of persecution was outside of the city walls on the north side of Mount Moriah. This was the same place where Stephen was stoned to death (Acts 7).

Jesus would have heard the priest blow the shofar (trumpet). He would have known it was 3 P.M., the time for the sacrifice of the Passover lamb—the time when the lamb's throat was slit and the blood was spilled and offered upon the altar to the Lord. When Jesus heard the trumpet sound, He said, "It is finished." Jesus chose the moment, the hour, the very minute to die. No man took His life. He laid it down Himself. Three days later He took it back and rose again from the dead.

The Passion

After the resurrection, Peter stated to a crowd of people in the Temple that "God before had [foretold] by the mouth of all his prophets, that Christ should suffer, he hath so fulfilled" (Acts 3:18). The prophets told of the Messiah, that He should suffer and rise again. It was the passion of God to become man, suffer, die, and rise again.

Approximately one hundred years after the Messiah's birth, Ignatius of Antioch, a disciple of the apostles, was carted off and led to Rome in chains. His crime? He was a believer in Jesus as the Messiah. As he traveled to Rome, he wrote letters to the first Christian churches. He spoke of many things regarding his faith and what he had learned from the apostles because he knew that when he arrived in Rome he was to be thrown to the beasts and martyred. He wrote, "Do not have Jesus Christ on your lips, and the world in your heart . . . I am yearning for death with all the passion of a lover."[1]

You see, his desire was to please God and to win the crown. He also stated, "All the ends of the earth, all the kingdoms of the world would be of no profit to me; so far as I am concerned, to die in Jesus Christ is better than to be monarch of earth's widest bounds. He who died for us is all that I see; He who rose again for us is my whole desire . . . Leave me to imitate the Passion of my God."[2] Ignatius was quoting Luke writing from Acts 1:3 referencing the resurrected Christ, "To who also he shewed himself alive after his passion by many infallible proofs . . . " Thus, we find the historicity of the term "the Passion."

When we think of the cross, we must remember the great cost of redemption. Though we may not fully understand as to why this was God's plan, or God's "passion," nevertheless, His plan is perfect.

Because of the death, burial, and resurrection of our Lord Messiah Jesus anyone who believes and turns to Jesus for salvation will receive:

1. Eternal life (John 3:16; 10:28)

2. Forgiveness of sin (Luke 7:47,48; Eph. 1:7)

3. Hope (Titus 2:13; Rev. 22:20)

4. Peace (John 14:27; Phil. 4:7)

5. Friendship with God (John 15:15)

6. Name recorded in heaven (Luke 10:20)

7. The hope of resurrection (1 Cor. 15)

The list goes on and on. You get the idea.

Jesus became our Passover Lamb, and at the right moment, by His own choosing, He died. Three days later He rose again.

---

1. Staniforth, *Writings*, 106.

2. Staniforth, *Writings*, 105.

What a blessed story! What a marvelous hope Christians have. May our hearts be stirred to live for Him who died for us and rose again. God's love is profound, and He wants to have a personal relationship with you, through His Son, the Lord Jesus.

Jesus was forsaken, so we, who believe, may never be forsaken. Jesus bore our sin and died, shedding His blood, so that we, who believe, may be forgiven. Jesus rose again, so that we, who believe, may have eternal life. *This is God's passion!*

"For God so loved the world, that he gave his only begotten Son, that whosoever believeth in him should not perish, but have everlasting life" (John 3:16).

— Chapter 10 —

Life After Death

Dedicated to Grandma Johnson! You loved Jesus, life and you loved me. You showed me how to live and taught me about the hope of eternity in Christ Jesus. I look so forward to hugging you once again—and having red Jell-O with you in heaven.

Preface

AS PEOPLE AGE THE question arises, "What happens after death?" What does occur when we breathe our last breath? This chapter addresses in a no-nonsense way what the Scripture states about death and the afterlife. This chapter is short enough to read through quickly and is chock-full of information that brings comfort to the one facing the last season of life. To demystify death and the continuation of life's journey on the other side of our present existence is a comforting reality that can be embraced intellectually, and emotionally, as well as spiritually.

What Happens Next?

Everyone will face the loss of a loved one in their life, and everyone will experience the loss of their own life. What happens when death occurs? Will I see my loved one again? Will I continue to live in another dimension? What comes after death? Is there a heaven (most people in the world believe in heaven)? What does heaven mean?

Destination

According to the Bible, the destination of all believers is the New Heaven and New Earth as recorded for us in Revelation 21. This is not some fluffy, cloudy, strumming harps, singing homogenous songs of ecstasy type of place. Rather it is a real place, in real time, with real people and celestial beings.

Trust

We can trust what God's Word states regarding the afterlife. We know we will be with loved ones. We know we will be with God. We know God has a plan. We know eternity is beyond anything we could ever imagine. We know the beauty and awesomeness will be profound regardless of how mind-numbing Hollywood has made heaven to be.

Number of Days (Ps. 139:16)

Living to be seventy years old, one will experience 25,550 mornings. That seems like a long time; however, over the years, a person begins to realize how swift, how precious, and how fragile each day really is. Knowing these things, we should create a point of reference in some form. For the atheist, these 25,550 mornings are a countdown to nothingness, to oblivion. The agnostic hopes for an afterlife—"We'll see what happens after the last breath" attitude. Concerning the afterlife, the apostle John writes, "Beloved, now we are children of God; and it has not yet been revealed what we shall be, but we know that when He is revealed, we shall be like Him, for we shall see Him as He is" (1 John 3:2). The point of reference for the apostle is that of an eternity with God in Christ.

Creeds

The Nicene Creed states, "And we look for the resurrection of the dead, and the life of the world to come." The Apostles' Creed records, "I believe . . . in the resurrection of the body, and the life everlasting." From the beginning, Christians looked forward to life everlasting.

There have been several books written about what heaven will be like; however, much of heaven remains a mystery—and mystery is good—for "eye has not seen, nor ear heard, nor have entered into the heart of man the things which God has prepared for those who love Him" (1 Cor. 2:9),

Gnostics

One reason that people believe that heaven will be a boring experience relates to the ancient Gnostic teaching that everything physical is evil and everything spiritual is good. To believe the Gnostics is to misunderstand the biblical teaching regarding God's creation. God called his creation "very good" (Gen. 1:31). Sin, however, has changed the dynamic of the universe and the status of human beings' relationships with God. God has promised to renew all things both physical and spiritual (Rev. 21) and Jesus came to pay the penalty for sin and the whole of creation is waiting for redemption (Rom. 8).

Glimpses

We have a glimpse of heaven in stories of profound love found between people and between people and pets; in the most beautiful awe-inspiring places on earth and in the multitudinous glories of the universe; and in the joy that a baby brings to the parents and grandparents. Any experience, good and beautiful, safe or warm, loving and kind, or anything you can imagine that can be summarized as good and joyful is only a glimpse of heaven (Jas. 1:17).

Raising All Things

Jesus said, "This is the will of the Father who sent Me, that of all He has given Me I should lose nothing, but should raise it up at the last day" (John 6:39). The Greek word translated "it" is a neuter pronoun meaning that Jesus will raise not only people but all things created (Rom. 8:19–22; Col. 1:20).

Everything Good

Everything good will continue—physicality of every creature; everything emotional; everything we sense on the earth and universe from breezes, fragrances, light, and aliveness. There will be work, learning, sciences, arts, and everything enjoyable (Gen. 2:15; 1 Cor. 13:12; Rev. 14:2, 3). God loves his creation and proclaimed it good, and creation itself is a mirror of God's magnificence and glory (Gen. 1:31; Ps. 19). Therefore, it is only natural to think that the renewal of creation will be part of our appreciation and activity of enjoyment in the afterlife.

Everything Bad

What will no longer be in existence is: evil, sin, and anything that is negative emotionally or harmful physically. No death, sadness, or hunger, and nothing representative of destruction, impairment, or mischief. No ecological damage, no mental illness, no pain, no grief.

Our emotions, which is very much part of being human, will experience a greater dimension of expression without the baggage of anything negative, painful, or sorrowful. Imagine only joy, compassion, and love. Imagine a fulfillment with complete gratification of experience and much, much more.

Mystery

Some things remain a mystery regarding heaven, and that is okay. Heaven is more than anything we could ever imagine. I'm not attempting to address all the incredible details about the afterlife, nor to grapple with the various interpretations of God's judgment(s), resurrection(s),[1] and all things future. However, there are a few colossal components we do know regarding what happens after our last breath.

1. Enoch & Elijah did not die, however, were translated (Genesis 5:24; 2 Kings 2:11) and some believe they are to be the two witnesses of Revelation 11:1–2 who will die and be resurrected. Some OT saints were resurrected (Matthew 27:51–52). Some Church saints were resurrected (Acts 9:36–41; 14:19–20; 20:9–10). There is the resurrection of Christ (1 Corinthians 15:20, 23); Resurrection of Life (Jn. 5:29); Resurrection of the Condemned (Jn. 5:29); More Church saints resurrected (1 Thessalonians 4:13–18, referred to as the "Rapture"); All OT saints resurrected (Revelation 20:4); Resurrection of the Wicked (Revelation 20:12–13); Judgment of Living Jews and Gentiles (Ezekiel 20:33–39; Matthew 25:31–46); Great White Throne Judgment (Daniel 12:2; John 5:29; Revelation 20:11–15); Judgment of Satan and Wicked (Revelation 20:14–15); and the Judgment Seat of Christ (2 Corinthians 5:10; Romans 14:10; 1 Corinthians 3:11–15). For complete information regarding God's judgments and the resurrections see: *Things to Come* by J. Dwight Pentecost (Zondervan, 1981).

1. Intermediate State

The idea of the Intermediate State is that we have complete consciousness after death (Eccl. 12:7; Luke 16:22-24). Between death and the resurrection of the body, something happens. Jesus said to the thief on the cross that, at the moment of death, he would be with Him in Paradise (Luke 23:43). The intermediate state is the condition of any individual, both believer and nonbeliever, immediately after death. A glimpse of this is found in Luke 16:22 where Jesus tells the story of a man who died and was with Abraham and of a man who died and was in torment. In this story, we find conversation and consciousness, both of which define the reality of continuing existence after death.

Paul stated that to be absent from the body (death) means that we will be present with the Lord (2 Cor. 5:8). There is no soul sleep as some interpret the Christian euphemism of "sleep" as found in 1 Corinthians 11:30 and 15:51. The word "sleep" simply refers to death. The body looks as though it is sleeping. The spirit has departed from the body, thus ending life here on earth. The bodily part of us appears to "sleep" until the final resurrection. Meanwhile, the spiritual part of us transfers to a conscious state of existence before the Lord. Apparently, this conscious state has some form of physicality, a form that is descriptive and recognizable. The Book of Revelation is replete with descriptions of individuals who have previously died being in a physical context before the final resurrection takes place (Rev. 6:9, 10; 7:10; 8:6, 13). The Book of Hebrews also points to physical descriptions of individuals in the intermediated state (Heb. 8:5; 12:22-23). It is clear that there will be a "spirit-type" of body between death and the final resurrection. The description is that of people wearing clothes, crowns, holding branches, and having body parts.

This place is not what Catholics refer to as purgatory. The belief in purgatory developed during the Middle Ages and became Catholic dogma at The Council of Trent (1545-63) as a reaction to the Protestant rejection of the teaching. One will not find the concept of purgatory in the Bible—only in the Apocrypha (2 Macc. 12:43-45).

Though much is speculation regarding the intermediate state, it doesn't, however, diminish the certainty of the hope of the *parousia* (Greek—second coming, or presence) of Christ in a new creation! After death, believers will experience Christ's presence (1 John 3:2-3) and ultimately the resurrection of their body to enjoy the New Heaven and New Earth.

2. Christ Will Return

According to Christ's answers to the apostle's questions as to what will be the sign of his coming and the end of the age, we find a decline in civilization rather than evolutionary buoyancy. Disasters in nature, horrid warfare, the redefinition of Christianity that leads to apostasy, and global human despair are found in Christ's description of world history leading up to the second coming (Matt. 24:3–27). Within this construct of time, a nefarious personality called the "the man of sin" (2 Thess. 2:3–4) or Antichrist will eventually hold the world in his sway until the second coming of Christ. At the second coming, Christ will not appear in a quiet little town in the West Bank—He will come on the clouds of heaven (Matt. 26:64) and, in so doing, crush the reign of the Antichrist. History will be altered once again because of this man from Galilee. The divine will reign supreme in the affairs of humankind.

It is not known when Christ will return (Acts 1:7). We know He will come as an unexpected thief (1 Thess. 5:2). We are to always be prepared for His coming, always expecting Him to arrive, and we are to "watch" for him (Mark 13:37). Therefore, we understand that his coming is *imminent*, it is always near, and there is always a tension of expectancy.[2]

3. Our Bodies Will Be Resurrected

We not only believe in the immortality of the soul but that one day our immortal souls will be reunited with our resurrected bodies—For the lover of God, a resurrection entering eternal bliss; for the rejecter of God, a resurrection unto eternal darkness.

At the resurrection, every part of our body will be raised, and not one hair will perish (Luke 21:18). The resurrection body is said to be a spiritual body (1 Cor. 15:35–46). This simply means our bodies will be released from the chains of a sinful-fallen state into a celestial existence. We will have the same qualities of Christ's human body on the Mount of Transfiguration and after His resurrection.

We will be recognizable as our corruptible must put on incorruption (1 Cor. 15:53), as this form passes away (1 Cor. 7:31) and we become eternally new—never growing old, no sickness, no pain, no sorrow (Rev. 21:1–5). Just as Mary recognized the resurrected Jesus' voice, our voice will

2. For more information regarding the various views on the Second Coming of Christ see: *Charting the End Times* by Tim LaHaye and Thomas Ice (Harvest House Publishers, 2001).

be recognized. Just as the disciples knew Jesus by the way he did things (folded napkin, throw the net on the other side, saying a blessing in Emmaus), so it is that we will be recognized by our loved ones because of the little idiosyncrasies we manifest in heaven. Jesus said of His resurrected body, "Behold my hands and my feet, that it is I myself; Handle me, and see, for a spirit does not have flesh and bones as you see I have (Luke 24:39)." *Handle me* suggests embrace. What an incredible moment that will be when we experience the celestial reunion of people we love.

4. There will be a Kingdom

Though Christ's Kingdom is beyond our full comprehension, we do understand a few details.

First, it will not be homogeneous. Within the kingdom, one will find diversity, the opposite of sameness. Like the Body of Christ today exemplifies an assortment of peoples, talents, and abilities, so it will be true in the kingdom. God will give each of us a "name" that only we will know (Rev. 2:17). The Lord will bestow upon both great and small responsibility and rest. There will be different rooms in God's house for His servants (John 14:2) which speaks of activity and special work in the kingdom. Just as there are servants with different statuses and work in kingdoms and governments today, so shall it be in the thousand-year reign of Christ (Rev. 20:4–6).

Second, there will be life to the fullest. The kingdom (and the New Heaven and New Earth which follows) shall not be a reclaiming of the original Eden as much as it will be a restoring and renovation, simply a renewed beginning, something that is greater than the first. God is infinite, implying a movement, a moving forward, constantly unfolding, not stagnation. Our soul belongs to God, and in the kingdom, we will still seek him. We will be in His presence, and yet He will be "Other;" we will bask in His glory and yet still have the need to grow; we will find rest and still be pilgrims; we will sit at His feet and still find mystery. As God continually unfolds and reveals Himself to us, we also continue to move straight ahead "from glory to glory" (2 Cor. 3:18), meaning the Christian experiences justification (forgiveness of sin), sanctification (living like Christ [Gal. 5:22–25]), and glorification (being in our resurrected body in His presence). However, we will never completely comprehend God; we will never exhaust His reality; we will forever be learning, ever growing in an eternity of God revealing Himself to us. Our journey will never cease. We will be more alive than ever before, beyond anything we could ever imagine.

5. Our Works Will Follow Us in the Afterlife (Revelations 14:13)

The word "rest" has the idea of freedom from weakness, failure, and the limitations we currently have in our body. In other words, we shall continue to be productive without the fragility of becoming tired or pausing, reinforcing the principle of moving straight ahead or that of progressive activity. Christ tells us that there will be the reward of more responsibility and gratification of self-worth (Matt. 24:45–47, 25:20–23; Luke 19:15–19). To the great will be given great and to the small will be given small—all will have worth and responsibility within the kingdom. Our life-work here is a preparation for bigger, on-going work there.

Jesus is our Shepherd and we will be like him. He has given us a paradigm to understand. The Scripture states that Jesus is the same in the past as He is today and as He will be in the future (Heb. 13:8). This being true, we can understand the principle in this manner: Jesus is the same "yesterday"—He was the Creator of the universe and all therein before He became flesh in Bethlehem; Jesus is the same "today"—on earth He was a carpenter, someone who works for others. He worked long hard hours. In heaven, He intercedes for us being the head, the chief cornerstone, of the church, and He is our Savior. Jesus is the same "forever"—as He will be the ruler, the king over His kingdom of multitudinous, busy, laboring, and serving, co-reigning redeemed people. Jesus puts it plainly when He states, "My Father has been working until now and I have been working" (John 5:17). He also said, "I say to you, he who believes in Me, the works that I do he will do also; and greater works than these he will do" (John 14:12).

6. We will be actively engaged in life in the kingdom

    a. Making decisions and interfacing with people
       (Matt. 19:28; 1 Cor. 6:2).

A judge, in a biblical construct, is a representative or ambassador of a nation, kingdom, tribe, or empire. Such a one travels, interfaces with other people, makes decisions, and alters the course of events. The implication is profound as one ponders that the One we are representing is the Creator of the universe and all things that exist. Our travels will be filled with splendid views and experiences of all things God has made. Have you seen the glorious Hubble Telescope photos? You will experience the universe with all your senses fully engaged, wide-eyed, with one-hundred-percent adrenalin. You will discover life-forms and beauty that presently we can only imagine. Oh, the wonder of it all.

    b. Dealing and conversing with angels (1 Cor. 6:3).

Think of it. We will be communicating with the vast, innumerable, variety of multitudinous celestial beings that are ever present before the Throne of God who have done God's bidding for millennia. We will know these glorious beings that protected Israel and the saints down through the ages. We will learn the details regarding how angels protected us in our life's journey. We will begin to understand the events surrounding eternity past and the mind of God as told by the seraphim, cherubim, archangels, and angels. Incredible!

    c. Assignments according to our love for the Master (2 Tim. 2:11–12; Rev. 5:10; Luke 19; Matt. 25).

To the degree, we identified ourselves with Christ here and now will be the degree of our eternal assignments. If we are faithful in little things, God will reward us with greater things. To honor the Lord with our "substance" (which generally refers to goods, assets, and money or material substance) was understood or commonly interpreted as meaning grace that was given by God, or to honor the Lord because of His love toward us. The motivation surrounding our love for God is predicated by God's love for us (1 John 4:19). God will honor those who fear Him (Ps. 111:5) with a single portion but will give a greater portion to those who are driven by love.

Paul stated that one should be strong in "grace" (2 Tim. 2:1) and that if we "die with Him" we shall also "live with Him" (2 Tim. 2:11–12) meaning our lives should be completely consumed and identified with Christ. A spouse will willingly give his or her life—give all for his wife or her husband, not out of fear but out of love. When a person loves another person, that one will be motivated to do more, to invest in the person he or she loves. In turn, the individual will receive blessing. So it was in the Parable of the Talents. Those who loved their master invested according to their ability, and at the end of the day when their "lord" returned, they received a greater blessing for their expression of love. However, the one who was "afraid" of his master and chose to be overly cautious, paralyzed with fear, and thus not moving forward and not willing to invest his time or ability received little or nothing (Matt. 25:14–30). So will it be in the kingdom of heaven. The reward will be measured by our love, not our fear.

7. Renewed Glory

The New Heaven, New Earth, and New Jerusalem is the finally re-deemed universe (Isa. 65:17; 66:22; Matt. 19:28; Acts 3:21; Rom. 8:18–21; 2 Pet. 3:13; Rev. 21:1–8). Isaiah, Jesus, Peter, Paul, and John address the renewed universe giving hope to all of God's creation.

There are two Greek words for new: *Neos*—something that did not exist before, therefore is new; *Kainos*—something that does exist, however it has changed. It is better, it is greater than before, it is enhanced, and it is superior; therefore, it is renewed, and its quality has changed for the better. When a person who believes in Christ becomes a "new man" (Eph. 4:24, *Kainos*), the quality of the person becomes better or becomes new. *Kainos* is used for the New Heaven, New Earth, and New Jerusalem in Revelation 21. The writer Isaiah uses a similar Hebrew word (*Chadash*) in Isaiah 65:17; 66:22. Simply stated, the universe will be renewed or reno-vated into a better or improved place.

In this divinely renewed universe, we will experience things beyond our finest imaginings. All things that were mentioned regarding the king-dom and things experientially immeasurable and incomprehensible will fully bloom in this renewed environment of creation. For those who love Him, God has prepared an eternity of discovery; a continuing of God's un-veiling of mysteries and wonders; a forever learning, growing, and joyous existence of understanding truth and meaning; never boring, never redun-dant, completely stimulating, and always fulfilling eternity.

Final thoughts and summary about what we know about the afterlife:

1. God will take care of you (Ps. 34:6; 91:4; Isa. 25:4; Rom. 8:37–39).

2. After our last breath, we experience consciousness in a spirit-body that has a recognized form: believers will be in the presence of God, nonbelievers will be in torment (Luke 16:19–31).

3. Christ will return and change the current state of humanity bring-ing universal peace, harmony, and justice and undoing the harness of lawlessness and evil.

4. Our bodies will be resurrected into a super-body, a glorified body like Christ's resurrected body. We will recognize each other and those who have gone on before us in death. Our actual bodies will come alive without the weaknesses and flaws we currently have. we will be new and strong, healthy and no longer tired (Job 19:25–27).

5. There will be a kingdom—"Thy Kingdom come" (Matt. 6:10). Within this kingdom, there will be tasks to be assigned and responsibilities to be handled. There will be activity and movement as people work together, seeking God, and living life to the fullest imagination. There will be animals in the kingdom (this would imply pets (Isa. 65:25)).

6. We will be able to continue our work and fulfill our hearts' desires (Rev. 14:13). We will finally be free from limitations that hold us back from fleshing out our full potential. We will be able to experience great accomplishment in the afterlife (John 14:12). Paul implies in Colossians 3:23–24 that we will continue with our talents and gifts as an act of worship to the Lord. Painters, scientists, musicians, athletes, carpenters, etc., will find uninhibited fulfillment and joy in their gifted areas of expertise.

7. We will eventually reside in a renewed version of the earth and universe with a beauty that is beyond present imagination and a forever stimulating experience of discovery and purpose. God in Christ will be the central focal point. To live in blissful rapture ever learning, ever moving, ever growing, everlasting—this is our future! *"For to me, to live is Christ, and to die is gain"* (Phil. 1:21).

— APPENDIX A —

Does God Care?

THIS PAST YEAR WE have found ourselves ministering to those in Israel who have suffered during the pandemic. Plus, more rockets are coming into Israel from Hamas's lair in Gaza and most recently Syria. School children race to bomb shelters when they hear the "red color" sirens sounding the alarm that rockets are falling from the sky.

Because of the stress and fear the children wet their beds and rock back and forth while sitting, not even realizing they are doing this motion. They have nightmares; parents weep and struggle because they have no money to buy food.

And there are *Holocaust survivors who live in poverty within the walls of Israel.* Among Israel's estimated 165,000 survivors, roughly one in three (or one-third) lives in poverty, according to a survivors' advocacy group. That's 54,450 survivors in poverty.

Obviously, most of Israel is doing just fine. However, the statistics show that *Over 2.5 million Israelis live in poverty, among them 1.1 million kids* (Timesofisrael.com, December 23, 2021).

The question is "Does God Care?" The early church fathers, both Latin and Greek, insisted upon what is called the "impassibility" of God. Basically, this means that while man experiences suffering, God himself does not. Yet, portions of the Hebrew scripture narrative imply God does have feelings and does react to suffering and pain.

Before Messiah, we find it stated of God:

"His soul could no longer endure the misery of Israel" (Judg. 10:16).

"Is Ephraim My dear son? Is he a pleasant child? For though I spoke against him, I earnestly remember him still; therefore My heart yearns for him; I will surely have mercy on him, says the LORD" (Jer. 31:20).

"How can I give you up, Ephraim? How can I hand you over, Israel? How can I make you like Admah? How can I set you like Zeboiim? My heart churns within Me; My sympathy is stirred" (Hos. 11:8).

It is stated of Messiah:

"And when He came near the gate o the city, behold, a dead man was being carried out, the only son of his mother; and she was a widow . . . When the Lord saw her, He had compassion on her and said to her, Do not weep . . ." (Luke 7:11–13).

"Therefore, when Jesus saw her weeping, and the Jews who came with her weeping, He groaned in the spirit and was troubled . . . Jesus wept. Then the Jews said, See how He loved him" (John 11:33–36).

"But when He saw the multitudes, He was moved" (Matt. 9:36).

Looking at these passages, if we learn anything at all, we learn that God is directly affected by the trials and anguish identifying with human pain and responding with immeasurable love.

God Cares

Our suffering causes God to grieve; God cries when we cry; God hurts when we hurt. This, of course, does not diminish who God is in terms of his essence, being all power, all knowledge, everywhere present. If human beings, created in God's image, can make suffering their own through their love for others, how much more can God, who is love, make our suffering His own?

In other words, if a human is affected by another's sorrow and pain, God is more affected. Why? God created us out of an act of love and is not indifferent to the angst we experience. He created us and is involved and identifies with us—even proving his involvement by taking it to the ultimate expression of love and concern—the cross.

Simply, God cries when someone dies; He has compassion on those who are ill; He sorrows for the children who do not have a meal; His heart yearns for the one gone astray; He has sympathy for those in need.

Our sorrow is mingled with joy because Messiah brings hope and answers in our time of need. God expressed his love through the life, death, and resurrection of Messiah Jesus. The resurrection proves that He is God. God is not indifferent to the sorrows of this world—and that brings an amazing comfort to my heart.

> *"Weeping may endure for a night, but joy comes in the morning"* (Ps. 30:5).

The Silent God

Why God Does Not Speak

"LORD, WHERE ARE YOU? I cried out to you over and over again. You have been silent! Where are you?"

Christians may face the challenge of God's silence. You know, when the hard times come—illness; financial difficulty; relationship problems; emotional challenges; spiritual depression; temptation. Where is God? Why is He silent? All believers in Jesus will face tests and trials somewhere along their journey.

Do you find, at times, when you cry out to Him that He is silent? I have.

When God reveals Himself, it is purely an act of grace through His Spirit. It isn't that God is silent. It is, however, that He chooses to reveal Himself to His children at specific times. When He does reveal His purpose in your life, it is usually very clear and sometimes suddenly.

Consider God appearing to *Moses* in the burning bush. It wasn't until Moses experienced an incredible season of trial and testing that God revealed His purpose (Exod. 3).

Look at *Elijah* after his victory on the mountain. He was exhausted and depressed, ready to die, and suddenly an angel touched him (1 Kgs. 19).

During a time of mourning, *Isaiah* was in the Temple and the Lord was revealed to him. His purpose was made clear. His path was set in motion. He now had clear direction and understanding of his circumstances (Isa. 6).

It was during a time of civil and political upheaval that young *Jeremiah* heard from God. God assured him that he was on this earth, this time, during this occasion, for a purpose. Jeremiah was set in motion once he understood from God why the times were the way they were. It now made sense to this weeping prophet (Jer. 1).

Ruth suffered the death of her husband and experienced great loss. She found God in the process and yet still suffered hardship until the Lord replenished her life with blessing (Ruth 1:16; 4:10–14).

Esther found that she was brought into the kingdom for such a time as this. What was this special time? It was a time of political turmoil in which the Jews would face extermination unless someone intervened. She found out that God orchestrated events in order to bring about something greater than herself. It wasn't an easy task before her. In fact, her life could have been taken from her if she failed. She prayed and asked others to pray. It worked, and God answered (Esth. 4).

The priest *Zacharias*, going about his daily duties in the Temple, was troubled when he finally heard from God. He and his wife were both righteous before Lord. They loved God and yet they had a test in their lives. Their burden? Elizabeth was barren, a curse in that culture. So, they prayed and prayed to God. He was silent for so long and then suddenly God spoke through the angel Gabriel. It startled Zacharias. In fact, he did not believe that God was answering his prayers. After all, it has been so long. Why now? He wasn't sure what to make of it all (Luke 1).

At the *Pool of Bethesda* there was a man with an infirmity desiring to be healed. He had this infirmity for 38 years. For almost four decades he suffered. He prayed and waited, prayed and waited. Then Jesus saw him. For almost forty years, there was silence. Then God appeared in the flesh (John 5).

Stephen, a man of faith, Spirit-filled, was living out his faith. He was put to death for his belief in Jesus. It wasn't until moments before he passed into the eternal that he saw Jesus and understood that he was in the perfect will of God, standing true to the faith (Acts 7).

Beloved, do you see a pattern here? Being a Christian, a follower of God, does not mean that you will be trouble-free. In every case, the believer experienced obstacles and valleys, and sometimes it cost them their lives. Months, years, decades, and then God speaks. It is then clear regarding the question "Why?"

To me, the propensity of God is to be silent. It is an act of grace and love. His silence strengthens our faith. "Faith is the substance of things hoped for, the evidence of things not seen" (Heb. 11:1).

Is God there? Yes! He is Emmanuel, God with us. You can see Him in the sidereal universe (Ps. 19:1). You can see Him in the gift of children (Luke 18:15–17). He is there in every breath you take (Acts 17:25). Every changed life is testimonial to the fact that God is there (2 Cor. 5:17). Every miracle points us to God (Luke 1:37).

Sometimes, we cannot see because our hearts are not clean. When we humble our hearts before Him and seek Him and confess our sin, He will cleanse our hearts and we will see Him (Heb. 12:14; 1 John 1:8–10). To seek the path of peace, holiness, and love is a difficult road. It is not natural for human beings to do so. It is only through His spirit seeking to follow His Christ that we shall see God, for Christ is God (1 John 4:4; Heb. 11:6).

1. Therefore beloved, when God is silent, remember He is there. He promised He will never leave nor forsake us (Heb. 13:5).

2. When God is silent, it is an act of grace and love to strengthen our faith (Heb. 11:1).

3. When God is silent, He has a greater purpose in mind, though we may not fully understand (Rom. 8:28–39).

4. When God is silent, the Spirit will make intercession for us, for we do not know what to pray (Romans 8:26–27).

5. When God is silent, we are to wait and hope for that which we do not see, nor understand (Romans 8:24–25; Isaiah 40:31)

6. When God is silent, do not despair, for at the exact moment, when the time is right, He will speak, and you will know what it means to seek Him.

"Shall not the Judge of all the earth do right?" (Gen. 18:25)

"Blessed be the Lord God of Israel for ever and ever. And all the people said, Amen, and praised the Lord" (1 Chron. 16:36).

Heart of the Gospel?

DURING SHABBAT, EARLY JEWISH *believers* would attend the temple, or synagogue, and pray the prayers, sing the songs, offer praise to God, and recite and read the Scripture only to realize all the liturgy was devoid of Jesus the Messiah. They could not worship the Lord in the synagogue or temple freely without resistance from non-believing Jews.

Shabbat worship in the synagogue or temple *excluded* the message that Messiah Jesus had come, died, and was *resurrected*. Early Jewish believers in Jesus did not want to disconnect from their holy traditions and Jewish culture. It was quite a dilemma for the early church.

The remedy was to keep the Jewish traditions on Shabbat (Friday evening until Saturday evening). Then on Saturday evening (which is technically Sunday morning, the day Jesus resurrected), they assembled. (How we got to Sunday morning worship is another teaching for another time).

Often, they met secretly, for fear, in homes continuing praying the prayers, singing the songs, reciting and reading Scripture. However, there was one big difference. Now they would *include* the worship of Jesus, singing songs about Him, and reading Scripture about Him, plus, the Lord's Supper or communion was observed each time they met (Acts 20:7; 1 Cor. 10:16–17, 11:17–34).

The reason for the persecution from the Jewish religious community, originally lead by Sha'ul of Tarsus, was not that they met to continue with the songs, prayers, and readings. The persecution was due to the fact that they began to worship Jesus. Jews were to worship only God. The idea of God becoming man was anathema to the Jewish religious mind. John wrote that Jesus is God. To worship a man as God was the trigger that caused the persecution.

Jesus is Lord

The reason they worshipped Jesus is because He rose from the dead. "If Christ has not been raised, your faith is futile; you are still in your sins" (1 Cor. 15:17).

The ancient church summarized the gospel in two Greek words: *Kyrios Iesous* meaning "Jesus is Lord." These two words direct us back to insinuations of deity and the exaltation of deity. When the early church heard or read those words, they recognized the connection to "HaShem" or "Adonai"—the Jewish way to say God.

The Greek word *Kyrios* is the same as the Hebrew word(s) *HaShem, Adonai,* or Lord. The Greek word *Iesous* is the same as the Hebrew *Yeshua, or* Jesus—"Jesus is Lord."

Not Disavow

The early church was persecuted because they would not disavow that Jesus is Lord. Therefore, both the religious and the Romans persecuted them, killing a multitude of believers.

Paul, who originally lead the persecution before his conversion, stated, "If, you declare with your mouth, 'Jesus is Lord,' and believe in your heart that God raised him from the dead, you will be saved" (Rom. 10:9).

The resurrection is the heart of the gospel. Any other message falls short. It is the core of what Christians must declare and believe to be saved.

Bibliography

Agnon, S. Y. *Present at Sinai: The Giving of the Law*. Philadelphia–Jerusalem: The Jewish Publication Society, 5754-1994.

Ahlquist, Diane. *The Complete Idiot's Guide to Life After Death*. Indianapolis, IN: Alpha, 2007.

Alcorn, Randy. *Heaven*. Carol Stream, IL: Tyndale, 2004.

Barclay, William. *The Gospel of John*. Volume 1. Philadelphia: Westminster Press, 1956.

———. *The Gospel of Matthew*. Volume 2. Philadelphia: Westminster Press, 1958.

Barnhouse, Donald Grey. *Genesis: A Devotional Exposition*. Grand Rapids: Zondervan, 1973.

Bell, James B. *The Roots of Jesus: A Genealogical Investigation*. Garden City, NY: Doubleday, 1983.

Bentorah, Chaim. *Hebrew Word Study: Revealing the Heart of God*. New Kensington, PA: Whitaker House, 2016.

Berlin, Adele, et al. *The Jewish Study Bible*. New York: Oxford University, 2004.

Bible Classics Devotional Bible: New International Version. Grand Rapids: Zondervan, 1996.

Bivin, David. *Dispatch from Jerusalem* 18.2. July/August 1993.

Blech, Benjamin. *More Secrets of Hebrew Words: Holy Days and Happy Days*. Northvale, NJ: Aronson, 1993.

———. *Secrets of Hebrew Words*. Northvale, NJ: Aronson, 1991.

Brenton, Sir Lancelot C. L. *The Septuagint with Apocrypho: Greek and English*. 1851. Reprint, Peabody, MA: Hendrickson, 2009.

Bruce, F. F. *The Gospel of John*. Grand Rapids: Eerdmans, 1983.

Chambers, Oswald. *My Utmost for His Highest*. Westwood, NJ: Barbour, 1963.

Clark, Mary T. *Augustine of Hippo: Selected Writings*. Mahwah, NJ: Paulist, 1984.

Criswell, W. A. *Expository Sermons on Revelation*. N.p.: Criswell, 1995.

DeHaan, M. R. *Adventures in Faith: Studies in the Life of Abraham*. Grand Rapids: Zondervan, 1953.

Edersheim, Alfred. *The Life and Times of Jesus the Messiah*. Volume 1. Grand Rapids: Eerdmans Publishing, Photolithoprinted, 1965.

———. *The Life and Times of Jesus the Messiah*. New York: Longmans, Green, 1910.

Elwell, Walter A. *Evangelical Dictionary of Theology*. Grand Rapids: Baker, 1984.

Fruchtenbaum, Arnold G. *The Book of Genesis*. Ariel's Bible Commentary Series. San Antonio, TX: Ariel Ministries, 2009.

Gaebelein, Frank E. *The Expositor's Bible Commentary: John, Acts*. Grand Rapids: Zondervan, 1981.

Gaer, Joseph, and Alfred Wolf. *Our Jewish Heritage*. Hollywood: Wilshire, 1967.

Galan, Benjamin. *What's So Great About Heaven*, Peabody, MA: Rose, 2009.

Geldenhuys, Norval. *The New International Commentary on the New Testament: The Gospel of Luke*. Grand Rapids: Eerdmans, 1979.

Goldstein, David. *Jewish Legends*. New York: Bedrick, 1987.

Harvey, A. E. *Jesus on Trial, A Study in the Fourth Gospel*. Atlanta: John Knox, 1977.

House, H. Wayne, and J. Randall Price. *Charts of Bible Prophecy*. Grand Rapids: Zondervan, 2003.

JPS Hebrew-English Tanakh. Philadelphia: The Jewish Publication Society, 1999.

Just, Arthur A., Jr. *Ancient Christian Commentary on Scripture: New Testament*. Vol. 3, *Luke*. Downers Grove, IL: InterVarsity, 2003.

Lach, Samuel Tobres. *A Rabbinic Commentary on the New Testament*. Brooklyn: KTAV, 1987.

Lahaye, Tim, and Thomas Ice. *Charting the End Times*. Eugene, OR: Harvest, 2001.

Leupold, H. C. *Exposition of Genesis*. Volume 2. Grand Rapids: Baker, 1964.

Lieber, David L. *Etz Hayim: Torah and Commentary*. New York: The Jewish Publication Society, 1999.

Lockyer, Hebert. *All About the Second Coming*. Peabody, MA: Hendrickson, 1997.

MacArthur, John F., Jr. *God With Us: The Miracle of Christmas*. Grand Rapids: Zondervan, 1989.

McGee, J. Vernon. *The Message of the Silent Years*. Pasadena: Thru the Bible Books, 1983.

Miller, Calvin. *The Book of Jesus*. New York: Simon & Schuster, 1996.

Morgan, G. Campbell. *The Gospel According to John*. Westwood, NJ: Revell.

———. *The Gospel According to Luke*. Westwood, NJ: Revell, 1931.

Morris, Leon. *The Gospel According to John*. Grand Rapids: Eerdmans, 1995.

Neale, Jospeh. *Commentary on the Psalms*. Volume 2. New York: Masters, 1868.

Novak, Al. *Hebrew Honey*. Houston: Countryman, 1987.

Pentecost, J. Dwight. *Things to Come*. Grand Rapids: Zondervan, 1981.

Phillips, John. *Exploring the Gospels: John*. Neptune, NJ: Loizeaux, 1989.

Pink, Arthur W. *Exposition of the Gospel of John*. Grand Rapids: Zondervan, 1975.

Plaut, W. Gunther, *The Torah, A Modern Commentary, Genesis*. New York: The Union of American Hebrew Congregations, 1974.

Prayers and Quotes taken from: https://billygraham.org/story/5-prayers-for-america-from-billy-and-franklin-graham/; https://www.faithandworship.com/ early_Christian_prayers.htm; https://www.gutenberg.org/ files/48247/48247-h/48247-h. htm#c3; https://ryanphunter. wordpress.com/2012/11/23/saint-anthony-the-great-on-guardian-angels/

Rice, John R. *The King of the Jews: A Verse-by-Verse Commentary, Matthew*. Murfreesboro, TN: Sword of the Lord Publishers, 1955.

Robertson, A. T. *Word Pictures in the New Testament*, Nashville: Holman Bible, 2000.

Rosen, Moishe. *Y'Shua*. Chicago: Moody, 1982.

Rozenberg, Martin S., and Bernard M. Zlotowitz. *The Book of Psalms: A New Translation and Commentary*. Northvale, NJ: Aronson, Inc., 1999.

Sarna, Nahum M. *Understanding Genesis: The Heritage of Biblical Israel.* New York: Schocken Books, 1970.

Scherman, Nosson. *The Chumash, The Torah: Haftaros and Five Megillos with a Commentary Anthologized from the Rabbinic Writings.* Brooklyn: Mesorah Publication, 2000.

Segal, Alan F. *Life After Death.* New York: Doubleday, 2004.

Spurgeon, Charles. *The Treasury of David.* Volume 1. Nashville: Thomas Nelson.

Staniforth, Maxwell. *Early Christian Writings.* New York: Penguin, 1968.

Stern, David H. *The Complete Jewish Study Bible: Insights for Jews & Christians.* Peabody, MA: Hendrickson, 2016.

———. *Jewish New Testament Commentary.* N.p.: Jewish New Testament Publications, 1992.

Swindoll, Charles R. *Exalting Christ, the Son of God: A Study of John 1–5.* Frisco, TX: Insight for Living, 1987.

Telushkin, Joseph. *Jewish Literacy.* New York: Morrow, 1981.

Tenney, Merrill C. *The Expositor's Bible Commentary: John.* Grand Rapids: Zondervan, 1981.

Thomas, W. H. Griffith. *Genesis: A Devotional Commentary.* Grand Rapids: Eerdmans, 1946.

Tittle, Ernest Fremont. *The Gospel According to Luke.* New York: Harper, 1951.

Vanderlip, D. George. *Christianity According to John.* Philadelphia: Westminster, 1975.

Vine, W. E. *An Expository Dictionary of New Testament Words.* Chicago: Moody, 1952.

Walvoord, John F., and Roy B. Zuck. *The Bible Knowledge Commentary: Old & New Testament.* Wheaton, IL: Victor, 1985.

———. *The Bible Knowledge Commentary: New Testament.* Wheaton, IL: Victor, 1983.

———. *The Bible Knowledge Commentary: Old Testament.* Wheaton, IL: Victor, 1985.

Ware, Bishop Kallistos. *The Orthodox Way.* Yonkers, NY: St. Vladimir's Seminary Press, 1995.

"Who's Who in the Bible." *Reader's Digest,* 1994.

Wiersbe, Warren W. *Be Loyal.* Wheaton, IL: Victor, 1980.

———. *Wiersbe's Expository Outlines on the New Testament.* Wheaton, IL: Victor, 1992.

Wilson, Marvin, *Our Father Abraham.* Grand Rapids: Eerdmans, 1989.

Young, Brad H. *The Parables: Jewish Tradition and Christian Interpretation.* Peabody, MA: Hendrickson, 1998.

Subject Index

Ancient Document Index

CPSIA information can be obtained
at www.ICGtesting.com
Printed in the USA
LVHW050555040323
740901LV00003B/10

9 781666 755749